Managing Boys' Behaviour

Related titles

Getting the Buggers to Behave 2 – Sue Cowley

Managing your Classroom, Second edition –
Gererd Dixie

100 Ideas for Managing Behaviour – Johnnie Young

Other titles in the Behaviour Management Series

Dos and Don'ts of Behaviour Management –
Roger Dunn

Managing Very Challenging Behaviour – Louisa Leaman

Managing Behaviour in the Early Years – Janet Kay

Managing Boys' Behaviour

Tabatha Rayment

continuum
LONDON • NEW YORK

Continuum International Publishing Group
The Tower Building   15 East 26th Street
11 York Road   New York
London SE1 7NX   NY 10010

www.continuumbooks.com

British Library Cataloguing-in-Publication Data
A catalogue record for this book is available from the British
Library.

ISBN: 0–8264–8501–4 (paperback)

Library of Congress Cataloging-in-Publicaton Data
A catalog record for this book is available from the Library of
Congress.

Typeset by Acorn Bookwork Ltd, Salisbury, Wiltshire.
Printed and bound in Great Britain by MPG Books Ltd, Bodmin,
Cornwall.

Acknowledgements

My thanks go to the following people for their help, advice and support while writing this book. Without them this book would not have been possible.

Julie Cole, Wendy Rayment, Graham Reeds, David Stevens, Melanie Teasdale and David Wood.

I wish to give special thanks to all the pupils and staff of

Billingham Campus School
Dyke House School
Nunthorpe Secondary School
Macmillan College

Contents

Contents

Contents

Introduction

At the beginning of my PGCE Teacher Training course at Durham University, one of my lecturers asked everyone in the class to write down on a small piece of paper why we all wanted to be teachers. He then advised us to put that piece of paper in a place where we could remind ourselves of our goals whenever the going got tough.

I still have that piece of paper stuck into the first page of my teaching diary. It says:

> 'I want to become a teacher, because I want to try and make a difference to children's lives.'

Even now sometimes, when I have had a particularly trying day, and the going *has* got tough, I will seek out that diary and read back what I wrote. It helps me to put things into perspective, and to remind me that although teaching can be one of the hardest jobs in the world, it can also be one of the most fulfilling, exciting and rewarding.

Introduction

My decision to write this book initially stemmed from research conducted into underachievement issues for a university assignment. The more I read about the issues, the more fascinated I became with the many different perspectives people in the education profession and the students themselves had about underachievement. Tired of reading mountains of data and hearing strategies designed by people who had obviously not set foot in a classroom for years, I decided to find out and document the *real* reasons behind underachievement.

This book was written for both PGCE/ITT students who are just beginning their teaching careers, and established teachers who have been in the teaching profession for many years. The student-based examples are taken from real experiences in schools where I trained and worked as a teacher.

Boys' underachievement is not a new phenomenon. It was first noted in the 1970s, but it was not until 1990 that any in-depth investigations were made into the issue. The apparent underachievement of girls in the 1970s and 1980s had sparked a change in examination procedures, which made them more friendly and accessible to girls. The National Curriculum was introduced in 1988; GCEs and CSEs were eradicated in favour of the new GCSEs, which meant more coursework and fewer exams.

This suited girls perfectly, as the emphasis was now placed on language-based learning and moved away from hands-on. As studies from the 1990s to the present day show, girls perform much better in areas such as coursework and language-based projects. For boys, however, this change meant that their acquisition of learning was made much harder. While the girls' achievement levels were satisfactorily raised, the boys' began to fall.

Achievement rates in today's education system are judged through examination results in national GCSEs and SATs, with a result of A*–C being a pass grade. Statistics and examination results are all very useful, and are indicative of pupil performance, but a grade or an award is only that. It proves a pupil's ability to perform under examination conditions. It says nothing of emotional or social intelligence, of their unique, personal skills or their long-term achievements.

A child only spends about 15 per cent of their time from the ages of birth to 16 in full-time education, and yet the education system is presented as if it alone is the sole source of all knowledge! Lessons, tasks and assessments are aimed towards getting good grades. There seems to be a very prevalent idea of 'if you don't get good grades, you won't go far in life'.

As a consequence, those who do not get the good grades feel like they are a failure, their self-esteem plummets, and their confidence in the skills they do have is seriously reduced. Without any clear direction available to them, and with the prevailing thought that they have failed before they have even begun, many boys fall into the trap of underachievement and poor behaviour.

This book is in two parts. The first part attempts to

explain the many contributing factors behind the rise of boys' underachievement. The second part looks at how we can create strategies to effectively raise achievement and successfully manage the behaviour issues often associated with underachieving boys.

I have included at the end of this book a list of further reading and recommended authors who focus on gender achievement problems and strategies to improve learning, which I found to be especially useful during my teaching and while writing this book. Some very helpful websites are also included in this list.

Part 1

Why Do Boys Underachieve?

1 The Spectrum of Problems

Boys' underachievement has been the focus of many studies over the years since the 1970s, and many people working in the education field have offered various theories as to the root of their misbehaviour, poor attitude and underachievement.

As adults, and professional educators, the whys and wherefores of misbehaviour and attitude problems in young boys can often be very frustrating, and it would be very easy to simply write off these boys as being 'bad' or 'vindictive'. When faced with 30 young students in a classroom environment, bad behaviour can begin to seem like the bane of any teacher's existence. Sometimes, all it takes is one or two individuals to 'play up' in class, and it can feel like all has become lost. It is a sad fact that behaviour issues appear to be much more problematic in our modern society than they were, say, 30 years ago. Teachers who leave the profession are frequently noted to cite bad behaviour as one of the key reasons for departing. More than a quarter of courses offered to professional educators to improve their teaching and learning skills focus on issues of behaviour management, with stress management being a close second.

However, although there can be little doubt that behaviour and attitude are problems in schools, I find it dangerous to put too much focus on them. It would be all too easy to brush off little Tommy's failing grades on his bad behaviour and attitude problem. A teacher who sits down in the staff room, bemoaning how they can't do anything with a particular student, or even, God forbid, proceeds to bad-mouth the student, is a teacher who really needs to reassess his or her teaching abilities. While I feel it is unfair to attribute bad behaviour to poor teaching, sometimes the buck really does stop here.

I am a firm believer in that no child is ever 'born bad', and that, however naive it may be, all children have at least one special talent inside them. It is up to us as teachers and mentors to unlock that potential and ensure every child gets the best possible start in life.

There are many imposing factors that affect child behaviour. To try and include them all in one volume would be impossible, but the key elements fall into five main categories:

- nature versus nurture;
- parenting;
- stereotypes and the media;

* learning styles;

* psychological, SEN and self-esteem issues.

Each of these headings contains a multitude of sub-headings and hundreds of different combinations based on the individual in question. There is no easy way to generalize and explain misbehaviour for all students. But, by gaining an insight into their background, upbringing and personal beliefs, it is possible to gain a deeper understanding of why underachievement and behaviour issues are a problem in some young men.

Underachievement and behaviour issues are a somewhat cyclical and connected problem. A student with behaviour issues is often an underachiever, and an underachiever often has behaviour problems. While there are some exceptions to this rule, I find it helpful to consider the two together when approaching the problems.

Every individual is different and unique. Between genetics and upbringing, we all acquire a completely original perspective on life and behaviour. Although generalizations can be made, each case should be taken on its merits, and a lot of behaviour management needs to focus on the individual as well as on the group.

Being a successful teacher is not easy. I do not know a single PGCE student who could walk into a school and instantly be an amazing and wonderful teacher. Similarly, I don't know of any experienced teachers who do not have a bad day occasionally. This is why teachers need to constantly and consistently reassess their teaching and learning skills to ensure they stay up to date on all the key issues and strategies. Teaching and learning should be synonymous, not just for the student but for the teacher as well. This only serves to strengthen the need for further training schemes and curriculum assessments for the entirety of the range of education provision, not just the pupils we teach.

2 Nature – Biological Differences in Males and Females

In an attempt to fully explain the exceptionally complicated process of learning, it is helpful to understand exactly how the brain develops before it can even begin this task.

Magnetic Resonance Imaging, a brain imaging technique, has considerably improved research into how the brain of each gender develops. Biologically, males and females are given a gender distinction by their genetic make-up.

Genetic Make-up

The nuclei of human cells contain 22 autosomes and two sex chromosomes. Female sex chromosomes are an identical pair labelled as XX. Males have one X chromosome and one Y chromosome. The presence of the Y chromosome is decisive for beginning the biological development programme that leads to a baby boy. There are some aberrations to this process, which lead to some genetic abnormalities, but all foetuses need at least one X chromosome, and the presence of the Y chromosome almost always defines the foetus as a male. In the initial six weeks of the foetus's life, there are no specific genitalia present. It is the production of specific hormones in the foetus that decides on the gender outcome.

Males and females produce the same hormones, but in different quantities. Males produce more androgens, particularly testosterone, while females produce more of the oestrogens. At the six-week point, testosterone production begins in the male foetus, which causes the embryo to develop as a male both physically and mentally. As before, some genetic abnormalities do occur which explains instances of hermaphroditism and physical and mental gender-orientated conflicts.

The Brain

Males tend to be born with bigger, heavier brains. This would explain the old, chauvinistic joke that males are brighter than females because they literally have more brains! However, intellectual capacity is not related to physical capacity. Instead, it is the complexity of the connections between the neurons (brain cells), that produces the overall intellectual capability.

Biological Differences in Males and Females

The human brain is constructed of four major parts: the brain stem, the cerebellum, the hypothalamus and pituitary gland (linked together), and the cerebrum. The cerebrum consists of the cortex, large fibre tracts (corpus callosum) and some deeper structures (basal ganglia, amygdala, and hippocampus). Each part has a particular role and controls specific functions.

The brain is separated into two halves, or hemispheres, which are connected by the corpus callosum, and information is transferred along these nerve 'highways'. Males have fewer links in the corpus callosum between the two halves of the cortex than females. This means that the two halves tend to operate more independently in males and more collectively in females.

So what does all this scientific information have to do with the learning process?

Through MRI research in developing individuals, scientists now know that the two sides of the brain function in very different ways. The left side concentrates mainly on logical and mathematical ideas, and the right side concentrates upon more visual, aural and emotive ideas. In addition to these findings, some scientists have suggested that different cerebral functions can be 'mapped' onto various areas of the brain. This is explained more clearly in the table overleaf. Consequently, as a result of this insight into the human brain, various theories have been forwarded to explain gender differences in learning processes.

Managing Boys' Behaviour

How the brain controls processes

The left side	The right side
Language processes	Patterns, shapes and forms
Logical thinking	Spatial awareness
Mathematical processes	Music and rhythm
Numbers and sequences	Visual stimulus
Analytical capability	Imagination
Random or unrelated facts	Connected learning

Storing Information

Current thinking suggests that boys are much better at spatial awareness and three-dimensional problems as they tend to favour the right side of their brains. This supports a widely accepted view that males are better at driving and map reading than females. Girls tend to use the whole of their brains and are much more successful at acquiring and using language, recalling things which concentrate on creativity or emotions, and understanding the 'bigger picture' of a specified task.

Boys are particularly competitive, while girls tend to share and cooperate more. It has been suggested that the higher levels of testosterone in boys make them physically more aggressive and assertive. Girls are more likely to persevere and complete a task, while boys have a shorter attention span and generally leave tasks unfinished. These characteristics, the scientists tell us, are not necessarily dictated by their upbringing, but are directly connected to gender pre-programming within the brain.

However, there are some problems with these ideas. If it were possible to localize specific areas of the brain to particular functions, then it would then be logical to suggest that if that area was lost, so too would the ability to perform the designated task. A random change in the brain might mean that a healthy individual would suddenly be unable to remember who they are or where they live.

Memories are not stored in the brain like files on a computer, instead they are spread out into a variety of areas and the brain accesses these simultaneously as they are needed. If the brain were designed like a computer hard drive, then the stored 'files' of information would have to be located and accessed by a scanning process. This in itself would use up both time and valuable resources. There may be a risk of the file being lost or corrupted over the process of time, from overuse or improper storage. The amount of space for storage might run out or suffer a hardware failure.

Human memory capacity is unproven, and we do not know whether or not there is an upper limit to what we can remember. No proof of reaching an upper limit has ever been found. However, that is not to say that this might not be possible, and that the amount of 'brain space' may differ from person to person.

The idea that certain functions could be 'mapped' onto the brain is certainly an appealing one, but humans are not biologically designed as neat, tidy, logical machines. A better analogy would be that of an eccentric professor's office. Some things are neatly stored away in filing cabinets while others are lounging on the desk stained with coffee-cup rings and biscuit crumbs. To the professor himself this system is perfectly acceptable, but to any outsider it may seem chaotic. Learning, it seems, just like a professor organizing his study, is an individual and unique process, that does not always follow any set rules of logic.

The Stronger Sex?

In Western society, males are generally seen as being the 'stronger sex'. They usually have more muscle mass than women; they are physically stronger, more aggressive, and are seen as powerful or dominant. Biologically, however, the idea that they are stronger is not true.

More male foetuses are conceived than female, and although exact statistics are difficult to find, it is estimated that around 25 per cent more boys are conceived than girls. Despite this, the male foetus develops much more slowly and is more susceptible to miscarriage. The process of testosterone production, which causes the male foetus to develop true male characteristics, also appears to disrupt the development process. Subsequently, male foetuses are usually smaller than females in the same time-scale of the pregnancy.

We know that male foetuses carry an X and a Y

chromosome. While the Y chromosome is indicative of gender, the X chromosome appears to contain information that is focused more on other foetal developments. Unfortunately, this X chromosome also seems very vulnerable to damage. While a female foetus still has the 'back-up' of another X chromosome, the male does not, If this chromosome becomes damaged, then the male foetus has a greater risk of developing infection and disease. As a result of this, they are also more vulnerable to problems that surround mental processes, such as autism spectrum disorders, ADHD or dyslexia. This genetic link, although still unproven, may explain why there are statistically more males than females with special educational needs (DfES research and statistics, 2004).

These genetic and biological differences offer some scientific explanations to gender differences in the learning process. However, they do not really give a definite answer to the question of why boys are seen to underachieve when compared to girls.

3 Nurture – Factors that Affect the Child's Development

After seeing how Mother Nature treats boys, it would be fair to think that biologically, boys get something of a rough deal. Not only are they slower to develop, they are at risk of being naturally aborted or of developing disease and infection while they are still in the womb. These complications continue for the boy after he is born.

Explaining how the effects of nature and nurture affect learning is difficult. It has been suggested that social conditioning and parental expectations can have a significant effect on how boys learn, and more importantly, how eager and interested they are to learn.

Behaviour Expectations

Modern society dictates some very clear ideas on how boys and girls are expected to behave. Deviating from what is considered to be the norm will result in ridicule and possible alienation from their peers. Gender distinctions have always been prevalent in society, with very definite ideas about how boys and girls should conduct themselves. The following traditional English nursery rhyme makes this very clear:

What are little girls made of?
What are little girls made of?
Sugar and spice, and all that's nice;
That's what little girls are made of.

What are little boys made of?
What are little boys made of?
Frogs and snails, and puppy-dogs' tails;
That's what little boys are made of.

The traditional idea of 'pink for girls, and blue for boys' enforces stereotypical gender distinctions on a child from the moment they are born. This trend is continued in the very different ways that parents treat boys and girls. While girls are expected to be demure, ladylike and delicate, boys are encouraged to be strong, adventurous and tough. While their parents protect the girls, boys are allowed to explore and learn from experience. Even crying is attributed to different reasons: in girls it is seen as a sign of distress, in boys it is a sign of anger.

It would seem that while girls are wrapped in cotton wool and protected in every way, the boys are left somewhat to their own devices to learn from their experiences. Boys are supposed to be tougher, stronger and can take care of themselves. A few hard knocks in the process of growing up are encouraged to strengthen boys even more. Although this is somewhat unfair for the boys, it is seen to be acceptable, as it is simply due to nature taking its course.

Unfortunately, the idea that boys should be tough continues all the way into adulthood. As the saying goes: 'boys don't cry' and any sign of weakness in a male is considered to be a bad thing. As a consequence, boys are not given much of an outlet to express their true feelings and emotions, and too much repression can lead to boys becoming much more aggressive and frustrated. Although girls are usually seen as the ones who throw tantrums, and strop if they don't get their own way, boys are often far more prepared to fight for it. Perhaps, before we put the blame on testosterone, we should take a good, hard look at how we, as parents and as a society, treat our sons.

Stereotypes and the Media

Advertising and marketing encourage parents to buy gender-orientated toys for their children. Girls are given dolls, home-based play-sets and beauty sets. From a very early age, these toys emphasize the idea that a woman's role in society is connected to being a home-maker and a mother. She is expected to think about her appearance and her behaviour, and model that on informed stereotypes she sees from immediate role models and from society.

Males, too, are expected to conform to the roles set out for them. Their toys are functional, practical and often mechanical. Boys are given cars and trucks, tool sets and heroic action figures. There are very few toys marketed that are not aimed at a specific gender.

Gender stereotyping is seen everywhere in mass culture. From pop videos to computer games, the media to advertising, the distinctions between genders are grossly exaggerated in many cases. Stereotypes are like codes; they give us an instantly recognizable and common understanding of a person or group of people. These usually refer to their gender, class, ethnicity, sexual orientation, their role in society or their occupation.

Almost all male stereotypes in the mass media fall into categories depicting their strength; either mental, physical or both. Men are often depicted as heroes who sport bulging muscles and fight for what they want, or they are the 'strong, silent type' and are academically brilliant business masterminds. The opposite of these are the 'geeks' or weaklings; these are seen as the runt of the litter and are the butt of jokes or looked down on. The media seems to suggest that if you are not big, strong, clever or aggressive in one form or another, then you are weak and worthless. Dominant masculinity is seen as the way forward.

However, there are also suggestions that society is becoming far more feminized. Macho roles are being questioned and rejected in favour of more delicate, feminine roles where it is acceptable to be in touch with your emotional side. As a consequence, males are left in a difficult position during their development where they have no strong male role models to guide them. While masculinity has traditionally been seen as superior to femininity, the change in favour of gender equality means that gender distinctions become blurred. For a young male coming to terms with his gender, this can leave him very confused.

As a result of the lack of any clear-cut stereotypes or role models, many young boys have to look elsewhere for examples on how to behave. Most young men will look to their fathers or dominant male figure in their family. For boys growing up in single-parent families, especially those who have no father figure, this is even harder. Even in those families who do have a father figure present, the media still plays a huge part in depicting how boys should behave.

What the media shows boys

From a very early age, boys are active users of the media, often much more than girls. They spend hours watching television, playing computer and video games, surfing the Internet and listening to music. Past research shows that these factors all have a very influential effect on young people, especially those going through adolescence when many crucial changes are going on in young people's lives.

Factors that Affect the Child's Development

♦ Emotions: Although male characters depicted in the media do show a wide variety of emotions such as anger, grief, pain and fear, it is very rare that they are depicted showing sadness or actually seen to cry. Men are almost always depicted as being strong, unemotional creatures that are more likely to fight than to break down. It is also very rare that these males are shown to give or receive any forms of non-sexual physical contact such as a hug.

♦ Violence: One in every five of male characters will use some form of violence to solve a problem, and anger is seen as a positive emotion. Males who don't fight are portrayed as being weak, and the fighting action is almost always a successful means to an end. In situations where men or their families or friends are threatened, a violent outburst or act of revenge is seen to be the best way of resolving the problem. The number of avenging or violent males is considerably higher than that of females, and it is usual that the male is in some way either protecting a female or dominating her.

♦ Work: The media invariably shows gender stereotypes with women being linked to domestic duties while men go out to work and bring in the primary income. Men are very rarely shown to do domestic duties such as washing up or vacuuming, and they are even less likely to be shown looking after children or babies while the mother works.

- Reality: Although most boys recognize the fact that the men they see on television are different from them, their families, and their social situation, many do not understand the reasons behind these differences and, as a result, they aspire to live up to what they see.

It is difficult to say how much of a deep, psychological impact the media has on young boys. Children learn a lot from copying behaviour they see around them. Programmes aimed at young boys are often of the superhero ilk, where powerful, muscled, and dominant males fight against evil every day. Boys, as nature dictates, are more likely to engage in some form of aggressive play, and the media simply caters for this. Computer and console games are six times as likely to be aimed at boys than girls, and the large bulk of these games involve some sort of violent or aggressive behaviour. Although these games masquerade under the pretence of good versus evil, justifying the violence does not make it any less violent.

Although it is easy to use the media as a scapegoat, it is not completely illogical to suggest that prolonged exposure to entertainment-based violence might breed real violent tendencies in impressionable young people. As a result, this has effects on their day-to-day behaviour and temperament and this is carried with them into schools. Not all children who play video games or watch aggressive television programmes will become violent themselves, but if children do indeed learn by copying, then they will not only copy good behaviour, but bad behaviour as well.

Extensive research into the effects of the media on children's behaviour and attitudes is largely inconclusive. In some cases, children who are exposed to high levels of aggressive stimulus will often chose to turn the other way and become exceptionally caring, loving individuals who abhor violence of any kind. In others, children who are never given the opportunity to experience violent media will suddenly exhibit aggressive behaviour without any obvious reason. It would seem that the media is a factor, but not a cause.

Gender Roles and Learning

If we consider how each gender is treated, and the role models society makes available to them, it is hardly surprising that by the time each child enters school, they are very different in terms of behaviour and attitudes to learning.

Consequently, it is the girls who are much better suited to formal education, while the boys start off strong but begin to dwindle as time progresses. While the girls appear to find reading, writing and arithmetic reasonably easy to grasp, boys often struggle, and even at this early age these feelings of failure can lead to some deep-rooted self-esteem issues.

To combat these negative feelings, boys often misbehave, 'acting up' to combat boredom and hide any obvious signs that they might not be achieving as much as is expected of them. Boys may be tough and strong, but underneath their hard exterior they are people too. While boys may appear to brush off bad experiences or are reluctant to voice their concerns, this doesn't mean that they do not care. No human being really wants to admit they are a failure, either to themselves or to others. Our self-esteem is very important to us. Human beings are naturally competitive; we want to do the best we can and achieve as much as we can, if for no other reason than to remind ourselves we have a purpose in life. To be a failure is to be weak, and, as boys are constantly reminded, being weak is bad.

Nature dictates that boys will be big and strong, their brains will ensure they are logical, practical and problem solvers. Their upbringing and nurturing enforces these ideas, ensuring that they live up to the expected masculine ideals. In prehistorical eras, men were the 'hunter-gatherers'. They protected, hunted and gathered food for their tribes. Their physical size, brain functions and their lack of ability to get pregnant meant they were designed for this role. Women were smaller and weaker; they stayed with the tribe, raised the children and were the healers. Through evolution, the successful male is bigger and more aggressive, and the successful female is the better carer.

In modern times, the gender roles have shifted, forcing males to not only be protectors, but also to be a source of knowledge and support, a role that they were not originally designed to do. There is little wonder that academic learning is not their strongest skill. And yet, the law says that boys and girls must receive some form of formal education up until the age of 16. They must receive the same structure of learning and attempt to achieve good grades in national examinations. When they do not achieve these grades, they are seen as failures. Their behaviour and attitude are considered to be a major problem, and they are constantly reminded of the fact that they are simply not as good or as successful as girls.

Peer Pressure

One of the strongest influences on children's behaviour, even more so than that of the media, is peer pressure. Children inevitably lead each other, and in cases where one child is more dominant than the other, they will often lead each other into negative as well as positive situations.

Children, and indeed, all humans, have an overriding and instinctual need for acceptance by their peers. While some people pride themselves on being outsiders, most are far happier to be part of a crowd and to be accepted into a social group. By the time children are attending school they are already shifting their orientation away from adults and towards their peer group. For boys, this means that a lot of stigma is attached to many aspects of their personalities and also in terms of their academic achievement.

Managing Boys' Behaviour

While media stereotyping enforces the idea of socially acceptable masculinity, being surrounded by large groups of male peers will ensure that the boy subconsciously attempts to conform to the set of behaviours and attitudes that are appropriately masculine. Thus he will become part of the peer group and will be accepted. Unfortunately for boys, gender stereotyping suggests that in order to be accepted you must live up to the prescribed roles, and these in turn do not advocate strong academic success. In order to be a 'real man', a boy is put under a lot of pressure to act in a 'laddish' way. There is a strong underlying sense that it is not 'cool' to be clever. Boys who are academically strong risk alienation from their peers, and as a consequence many are ridiculed or bullied. It is only if they attend a school with a positive study ethos or if they are good at sport that they can avoid this.

Sometimes it is not the fear of alienation that spurs boys into following their peers, but part of their natural curiosity. When faced with the idea of 'everyone else is doing it', it is often very easy to get drawn into particular situations that they might not otherwise actively seek out. Experimentation is a natural part of growing up and developing, and experience is a powerful educator.

In addition to this, boys very often have a 'pack' mentality where there is safety in numbers and they can be accepted into a social group. If their peers in these groups have a strong dislike for the education system, it is likely that they will adopt this too. Boys often feel that their masculinity is something that they must constantly prove and affirm. Many boys believe that the best way of doing this is to seek guidance and advice from their peer group. A quarter of the boys I spoke to in schools said they have bullied or been bullied due to the 'swot' syndrome. This enforces the idea that 'real men are not swots', and being an academically high achiever is not something to openly aspire to.

While girls seem to derive enjoyment out of learning and gaining rewards for their achievement, boys shrink away from this. Their argument is that it is not masculine to be clever, and they would far prefer to be rewarded for achievements based on their physical strength. For those boys who come from 'tough' families or are part of gangs, gaining high grades means social suicide and possible alienation from their peers.

However, not all peer pressure is bad. Positive peer pressure can ensure that bullying can be stamped out or unwanted behaviour can be neutralized. A child who 'plays up' in class will soon stop when he realizes he does not have an appreciative audience. In some lessons I have taught, some 'problem' students often tried to disrupt the education process. When the other members of the class failed to support him or have told him to be quiet, the effect was far more successful than any of my disciplinarian efforts!

As professional educators, we cannot realistically eradicate the influences of the media and peer pressure on our students. If we provide students with positive, unbiased role models we can potentially create a more stable and open-minded learning community. However, children will always learn from what they see and whom they interact with. It is essential that children be allowed to make their own discoveries and mistakes during the process of growing up. If we guide them too much, then they may not develop their own independence.

Boys are not naturally suited to the academic process, and after looking at the effects that nature and nurture have on their development, it is easy to see why. Perhaps in the future, instead of hearing the old and overused excuse of 'the dog ate my homework', we may begin to hear a more truthful, 'I'm sorry, I couldn't do this. It's because I'm a boy.'

4 Parenting, Poverty and Behaviour

Parenthood is never easy. For some, parenthood comes naturally, almost as if they were born to be mothers or fathers, but for others it can be a struggle to know what to do, how to cope and to know how best to bring up their new arrival.

Parenthood carries with it a huge amount of responsibility; the child needs to be looked after for almost 18 years. Parents don't get a day off; they are Mum and Dad 24 hours of the day, seven days a week, 365 days a year. They are role models, providers, advisors, disciplinarians and carers; and they are expected to perform all these duties while showing unconditional love to their child. It is an exhausting and confusing experience, but, like teaching, it is also highly rewarding.

Living in Poverty

One of the most crucial questions of all, and something that many parents often ask themselves, is: 'what makes a good parent?'

Obviously, taking good care of the child and ensuring they have what they need is the first and foremost necessity. Cleaning, feeding, supporting and guiding are all very important roles that a parent plays. Just as important as these, however, is the way a parent brings up a child, and the ideas and lifestyles of the parent are likely to become the ideas and lifestyles of the child.

How much can we blame bad parenting and social factors on boys' underachievement?

In 1994, Harry Enfield and Kathy Burke portrayed the characters of Wayne and Waynetta Slob, a pair of uneducated and foul-mouthed characters who lived up to their name. The Slobs dress their beloved offspring, who are rather unfortunately named Frogmella and Spudulika, in mock-designer gear. Their names are allegedly 'exotic'. When their teacher tells him his children have Special Needs, Wayne honestly believes she is referring to their love of junk food and chocolate, not to their genetically inherited educational deficiencies. The Slobs are unemployed and live on state benefits. Their standard of living is low and they have few, if any, qualifications. Sadly, it seems that some areas of Britain have a good percentage of homes and people identical to that of the Slobs.

Figures published by UNISON and the National Statistics website reveal that:

◆ Unemployment levels in Britain stand at 4.7 per cent with 1.41 million people of working age (16–65) not in any gainful employment. Males make up over 60 per cent of the unemployment figures, with the highest numbers in the 24–49 age group (32 per cent).

◆ The national average weekly income of a household in Britain is £475.80, but individuals living on state benefits receive on average only £53.95 per week to cover everything other than housing and council tax costs.

◆ For people in impoverished areas, the pressure to find a job is increased. Many young people leave education at 16 to join the labour market. Their lack of advanced qualifications often means they can only secure unskilled or manual labour work earning the national minimum wage – £4.85 per hour at age 22 and over. In a job of 40 hours per week, this means that their gross weekly income is only £194.

◆ Forty per cent of children in the UK are born outside of marriage, with 7.5 per cent of children born to mothers between the ages of 15–19.

◆ It is estimated that one in three British children, almost 4 million individuals, are living in poverty. Eighteen per cent of poor children go without two or more items that are considered necessities for living, such as adequate clothing, toys, or three meals a day.

People who live in poverty generally do so together due to social and economical factors, and as a result this often only serves to make the issue worse, with the standard of living being particularly low.

Continuing the Cycle of Underachievement

Returning to our original question of parenting, what happens when a child is born into a family that is part of these national statistics? Subsequently, what effect does this have on his or her achievement at school?

Learning is highly contagious. If a child is born into a family with high levels of intelligence, chances are that they too will be academically successful. Unfortunately, this also goes the other way. Parents who did not do well at school often raise children who also do not do well at school. In many instances, families living in poverty are not high academic achievers. Obviously, as with all generalizations of this kind, there are always exceptions to the rule, but overall this is a very common trait.

A lot of the underachievement we see in boys today is a result of second or third generation underachievement. Unless something is done to raise these levels, it is a trend that is likely to continue well into future generations for years to come. As standards lower and grades decrease even more, the overall level of achievement in society is following a downward spiral into academic decline. The boys we teach in schools today are the parents of the future, and the education they receive now is the education they will pass on to their children. It is a terrible shame that strategies and implementations in the past have not done nearly enough to raise boys' achievement levels, and as a result we are looking at more and more young men who will follow in their fathers' footsteps, often to the unemployment line.

Parenting, Poverty and Behaviour

Surprisingly, however, 88 per cent of the boys I asked during my research into underachievement said it was their fathers who helped them with their homework. Sometimes this was because they thought their fathers were more clever, sometimes it was due to their mothers being too busy. Whatever the reasons, there was no evidence to suggest that fathers weren't taking an interest in their sons' education.

I believe this to be a highly encouraging finding; it means that even though boys have been underachieving for many years, they have not completely dismissed the education system. Taking into consideration that a lot of these boys' fathers are some of the first generation of underachievers, and despite the fact that their sons are also underachievers, taking an interest in their sons' education is a good sign that poor parenting or poverty isn't always to blame for academic problems.

Discipline in the Home

Although fathers do seem to be taking some interest in their sons' education, the same cannot be said for their behaviour and attitude problems. In one of the schools I worked in, certain parents were banned from entering school grounds due to their poor attitude and sometimes violent or aggressive behaviour towards school staff. In some cases, if problems arose with a student, teachers were advised to contact a social services representative rather than the parent directly. It comes as no surprise to find that their children also showed signs of violent, aggressive and antisocial behaviour.

Some parents, often those from deprived social and economic areas, seemed totally disinterested in their sons' behaviour problems. One parent even went so far to suggest that his son's penchant for bullying and physically attacking other students was just a sign that 'boys will be boys'!

During my research I asked 40 underachieving boys a very delicate question: was their father or prominent male in the household ever verbally or physically aggressive either to them or to other members of the household? I was shocked to find that a quarter of the boys said that their fathers had physically punished them, and a further 10 per cent said that they often saw their parents verbally or physically fighting. Encouragingly, however, all of the boys agreed that violence, especially towards women, was definitely wrong, and the boys were particularly protective of their mothers and sisters. When asked if violence itself was wrong, only 80 per cent said yes, with the rest saying that sometimes violence is acceptable in some circumstances. It stands to reason that if a child is exposed to this kind of behaviour in the home, then he will carry it with him into the school.

Discipline, it seems, was something of a grey area to these boys. Over half of them said that the main disciplinarian in the family was their mother, but it was their fathers who were more likely to 'give them a smack' if they were 'out of order'. Curfews were few and far between, with just under half of boys saying they 'went home when they felt like it' and there was no definite time for them to be home on an evening, even during a school term. Evenings were usually spent either in their rooms playing on computers or games consoles, watching films, or on the streets with their mates, just 'hanging about'.

Some of the boys admitted to being part of some kind of gang, their nightly activities included riding around on bikes, experimenting with tobacco and alcohol and just general talking. They did not see a problem with their behaviour, and thought that street curfews were just 'people trying to stop [them] having fun'. The 'gangs' varied in size from approximately four to six youths up to gatherings of 'about 20' sometimes. The boys did understand why these groups might be seen as intimidating by other members of society, but insisted they 'weren't doing anything wrong'. It was impossible to say if their parents knew about their nightly activities, but it would appear that the lack of curfew or direct discipline showed some disinterest on the part of the parent.

Chav Culture

The Oxford English Dictionary recently added the word *chav* to their list. A Chav, or a Charver (optional spelling: Chava), is defined as a young person, often without a high level of education, who follows a particular fashion. The government often refers to the younger generation of Chavs as NEDs – Non Educational Delinquents.

Chavs do get a lot of bad press, and much of this relates to social stereotyping. The media often paints a picture of Chavs being antisocial, aggressive and violent. They are seen as being unsavoury, troublesome members of society. However, being labelled a Chav does not necessarily mean that person is bad. Much of the Chav culture is based around the fashion and music they follow. Just like the Teddy Boys, Mods and Rockers, Hippies, Punks and New Romantics, Chav is just another youth movement, a way of defining oneself in the modern world. However, Chav culture often brings with it the problem of lack of education and underachievement.

Children who leave school ill-equipped to lead satisfying, healthy lives often get involved with crime, drugs or other forms of substance abuse. The notion that education has done nothing for them and it was a waste of time for them becomes passed down to the next generation, and eventually a vicious circle is formed. Chav families generally produce Chav children, and that, in turn, continues the decline of education and academia. While the media may focus on celebrities such as Danniella Westbrook or Wayne Rooney being 'Chavs', the reality is one of poverty, social deprivation and a lack of real education and employment prospects.

Chav culture is not an exclusive factor to underachievement, but it does have an impact. Chav parents are also not *bad* parents. All they are trying to do is raise their children with the same moral and ethical views as themselves, just as any other parent does. Their lack of interest in the education system is understandable. To these people the education system is one that labelled them as failures and released them into a society where they cannot hope to excel. Unfortunately, this attitude does nothing to stop the cycle of academic decline and lack of value in the education system. Without significant change somewhere, Chav culture, and underachievement, will continue to be synonymous for generations to come.

Truancy, Crime and Behaviour Influences

In the UK the law says that all children must be given some form of legally recognized education from the first school term after their fifth birthday up until the last Friday in June of the year they turn 16. The law says that a child's parents or guardians are responsible for making them attend school, unless the child is officially educated at home. Parents who do not do this may receive fines or prison sentences if their children are constantly missing from the education system.

It is estimated that somewhere in the region of 50,000 students are absent from school without permission. This makes a total of 7.5 million days being missed annually. Missing out on school, even only occasionally, has some severe implication on a student's learning and achievement. Even one day missed here and there can mean the student misses out on an important part of his or her education. Students may fall behind, and the pressure is increased on teachers who have to find time to repeat lessons to help the student catch up.

Government studies suggest that those children who play truant are more likely to commit some form of criminal offence compared to those who do not truant. It is estimated that 65 per cent of young offenders are also truants. Only 10 per cent of persistent truants achieve five good GCSE grades of A*–C and approximately a quarter of these stay in full-time education over the age of 16. Another quarter of these is unemployed after leaving school.

Truancy is approximately four times more common in boys than in girls. There is little doubt that the number of missed days at school is having a large impact on their education as a whole, and contributing to boys' underachievement. Many of the boys I spoke to said they could not see how much of what they did at school was going to help them in later life. 'Boredom' and 'pointless tasks' were cited as being the main reasons for poor behaviour and playing truant. 'Peer pressure', and 'everyone else does it' were other reasons for going AWOL from school.

Under British law, offenders under the age of 18 get very little punishment for bad behaviour, and in turn, many of these children see themselves as untouchable. Although Anti Social Behaviour Orders (ASBOs) have massively cut down incidents on the streets in many areas of Britain, and some boroughs have imposed juvenille curfew orders on children under the age of 16, crime levels in minors still continue to rise.

Government statistics indicate that 90 per cent of juvenile offenders under the age of 16 come from broken or one-parent homes, and more than half of these have been excluded from school. The cost of juvenille crime in the UK is estimated to be over £18 billion a year, with a large chunk of this money being spent on providing care and support for young offenders, many of these being young males. That money could be put to far better use improving the education system and stopping the problems before they arise. Currently, the UK government spends almost £55 million across the education and skills system, but it seems that this spending is not enough.

Studies in psychiatry and psychology frequently show a strong link between parental behaviour and that of their children. Much of children's misbehaviour and attitude is influenced in the way that their parents behave towards them. In many familes with antisocial children, the parents concentrate too much on discipline and forget to reward good behaviour. In this situation, only bad behaviour or tantrums get the attention results the child is seeking.

Long-term behaviour problems can be linked to five areas of 'bad' parenting:

1. Poor or inaccurate supervision of the child.

2. Poor discipline or over-harsh discipline measures, which includes physical punishment.
3. Lack of harmony in the parental home such as arguments, antisocial behaviour from the parent and no moral or ethical values upheld.
4. Lack of involvement in the child's life and no interest in their achievements or sucesses.
5. Some form of rejection of the child where the child is made to feel unwanted or unloved by their parents.

To combat behaviour disorders and help raise the self-esteem of the child, work needs to be done with the parents when the child is still young.

Can We Really Blame the Parents?

Poverty and a lack of opportunities for young people do contribute to the decline in achievement, but they are not the root cause. Many young individuals from deprived and one-parent homes do not turn to crime or violence and a good percentage go on to lead happy and fulfilling lives.

The quality of relationships available to them at home and within their familes will have a huge influence on a child's ability to get what he or she can out of life. Having a good support unit will ensure that the child faces and overcomes any challenges that poverty and deprivation raise. If a child comes from a background where education is neither encouraged or valued, it has a significant impact on their thinking from a very young age. A major factor in a child's success in the education system is the encouragement and support they receive from their parents. If that support is not there, then the child is less likely to value their education, and as a result, will become another addition to the list of under-achievers.

A good parent is an interested parent, a parent who will provide guidance and support and encourage their child to do better than them. I have never heard of a parent who did not want the best for their child, but it is a sad fact that sometimes parents do not realize that they could do more to encourage this. By etching into our children our own ideas and views, sometimes we can do more harm than good.

Part 2

What Can I Do About It?

5 Teaching and Learning Styles

> I hear and I forget,
> I see and I remember,
> I do and I understand.
> Confucius c. 450BC

Within the last twenty years, there has been a marked increase in our knowledge of the ways in which humans develop and learn. Scientific research shows that babies are beginning to learn even before they are born.

Just as not all individuals have identical personalities, not all individuals learn in the same way. Every child is unique in his or her personality, cultural experience and values. Different students prefer different learning environments and learning modalities, and they all exhibit unique strengths, talents and/or weaknesses.

Learning Styles

Many psychologists and educational theorists have offered reasons as to why some children prefer certain learning styles to others. Howard Gardener in his book *Frames of Mind: The Theory of Multiple Intelligences* identified individual talents or aptitudes through multiple intelligence theories. These suggested the idea that there are eight main intelligences (see table). The Type Indicators, Sorters and Delineators of Karl Jung, David Kolb and Anthony Gregorc follow a similar approach.

The eight learning styles

1 Linguistic	Enjoys writing, reading, telling stories or doing crossword puzzles.
2 Logical	Interested in patterns, categories and relationships. Drawn to arithmetic problems, strategy games and experiments.
3 Kinaesthetic	Processes knowledge through bodily sensations. Often athletic, dances or good at crafts such as sewing or woodworking.
4 Spatial	Thinks in images and pictures. Often fascinated with mazes or jigsaw puzzles, or spends free time drawing, building with blocks or daydreaming.
5 Musical	Always singing or drumming to themselves. Usually quite aware of sounds others may miss. These children are often discriminating listeners.
6 Interpersonal	Leaders among their peers, who are good at communicating and who

	seem to understand others' feelings and motives.
7 Intrapersonal	May be shy or stubborn. Very aware of their own feelings and are self-motivated. May keep a journal, express strong emotions and have well-developed opinions.
8 Naturalist	Has a good ability to recognize and classify elements of the natural world. May be fascinated by all kinds of creatures and animals.

All these styles approach learning in vastly different ways, but all have some value when investigating children's learning styles. Children develop in very similar ways in four key areas: physically, mentally, socially and emotionally. The activities and experiences that a child is exposed to from birth to ten years will have a radical impact on the child's development into adulthood. As children interact with their environment, they learn problem-solving skills, critical-thinking skills and language skills.

Rita and Kenneth Dunn in *Learning styles: Theory, research, and practice* (2000) argue that the more positive the stimulus, the more positive the reaction and development of the child. Their learning style model is based upon five different strands of 21 different elements.

- Environmental strand: Focuses on lighting, sound, temperature and positioning. A comfortable temperature, soothing music and sufficient light are all factors that may attribute to better learning.

- Emotionality strand: Looks at the personality of the learner, their motivation, persistence and responsibility.

- Sociological strand: Represents elements related to how individuals learn in association with other people: alone or with peers; with an authoritative adult or with a collegial colleague; and learning in a variety of ways or routine patterns.

- Physiological strand: Concentrates on perceptual elements, energy levels, intake and mobility. For example, some people feel they perform better in the morning or have to take regular breaks while studying to prevent becoming restless.

- Physiological elements: Correspond to left and right brain processing, the nature and nurture influences that affect an individual's learning style. These are global and analytical elements that are clusters of the other four strands.

As we already know from studies in genetic development, girls are naturally predisposed to be well suited to formal education. As a group, boys tend to learn less by listening, more by doing and seeing, and they are more nonconforming and peer motivated than girls.

Girls, more than boys, learn by listening, and they are often more conforming, authority-oriented, and better able to sit passively at conventional desks and chairs. While girls are more dedicated to a task, boys will frequently become bored and leave things unfinished. Consequently, this may be perceived as a lack of motivation or deliberate disinterest, but the reality is that gender differences play a very important part in student's learning styles.

David Kolb and Anthony Gregorc developed their Type Delineator to assess how the individual's personality affects their learning capability. Kolb (1984) explored the concept of cyclical and experiential learning. He found that the four combinations of perceiving and processing determine four learning styles. The learner goes through four stages:

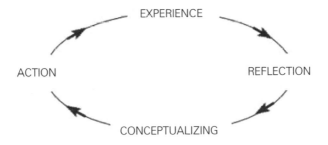

The cycle is completed with the learner going on to gain further experience.

Kolb's diagram describes the process for recording continuous professional and academic development, and proves that learning is a continuous process regardless of age or ability. It was Peter Honey and Alan Mumford (*The Manual of Learning Styles*) who later defined four styles, based loosely around the four stages of Kolb's cycle:

1   Activists
2   Reflectors
3   Theorists
4   Pragmatists

Activists are people who learn by doing. They need to experience learning firsthand to truly understand and appreciate what it is they are attempting to find out.
Reflectors learn by observing and thinking. They watch from the sidelines and attempt to gain as much information as possible before starting a task.
Theorists need to understand the theory behind the task. They need rules and logical structures to ensure they fully understand.
Pragmatists need to see how their learning can be put into practice in the real world. They are easily confused by abstract ideas unless they somehow fit into a bigger picture.

Although each individual will be more adapted to one particular learning style, research suggests that in order to be a truly effective learner it is necessary to develop the ability to learn in other styles too.

Visual, Auditory and Kinaesthetic Learning Styles

Research has shown that boys do not do well with language-based learning or writing things down, and instead they learn by different stimulus. A lesson, which incorporates visual, auditory and kinaesthetic styles, is more likely to be satisfactory when aiming to raise boys' achievement in the classroom. Teaching presented through large amounts of reading and writing is more likely to make a boy 'switch off' than if he can see, hear and feel what he is supposed to do.

Coupled with setting attainable and realistic targets, using the Visual, Auditory and Kinaesthetic (V.A.K.) method of teaching will help boys to become more involved in their work and thus achieve more. The following table shows the characteristics of V.A.K. learning styles.

	Visual	Auditory	Kinaesthetic and tactile
Spelling	'Sees' the word.	'Hears' the word or uses phonetics.	Writes the word down and sees if it feels right.
Talking	Talks a little but dislikes listening for too long. Words such as: picture, see, imagine, are favoured.	Enjoys listening but get impatient to talk and often interrupts. Words such as: hear, tune, think, are favoured.	Uses lots of gestures and expressive movements with the hands and face. Words such as: touch, feel, hold are favoured.

	Visual	Auditory	Kinaesthetic and tactile
Concentration	Untidiness and movement are a distraction.	Sounds and loud noises are a distraction.	Activity of any kind is distracting.
Reading	Favours descriptive scenes. Can imagine and picture the action.	Dialogue and conversation are preferred. Can 'hear' the characters talking.	Action and adventure is preferred, but as a general rule does not read much or often.
Doing something new	Likes to see demonstrations, diagrams or posters that show how it should be done.	Prefers verbal instructions or to talk about it with someone else.	Jumps right in and tries it out.
Putting something together	Looks at directions or pictures for guidance.	Asks for help or talks about it with others for guidance.	Ignores directions and tries to figure it out as they go along.
Meeting people	Frequently forgets names but remembers faces.	Forgets faces but remembers what has been talked about.	Remembers best the kind of activities done together.

Putting Learning Styles into Practice

With all this scientific and philosophical information available concerning learning styles, actually putting these theories into practice in the classroom can prove to be confusing and problematic.

How can a teacher know what kind of learners he or she has in their classroom? How can they possibly cater for such a wide variety of contrasting styles and still maintain the flow and pace of the lesson?

The easy answer of course is to consider differentiation techniques. The harder answer would be to conduct considerable research into every student's learning background and behaviour and attempt to modify teaching styles to accommodate every student.

More often than not the classroom can become a very male-dominated place. Aggressive and assertive males frequently demand teacher attention through misbehaviour and unwillingness to learn. As a result the teacher may feel he or she is spending more time attempting to address behavioural issues than teaching a lesson. This in turn affects the female members of the class who are not given a proper opportunity to involve themselves in the lesson. Although this may appear to be linked more to classroom management strategies, it is also an ideal situation to assess how each individual learns in this environment and develop strategies to improve both teaching and learning.

Firstly, a teacher should show enthusiasm for his or her subject. It would be impractical and unrealistic to allow a teacher with low motivation and poor preparation to teach any student. Excellent lesson planning and a good knowledge of the subject is the first step in addressing any teaching and learning issues, and will have a considerable positive impact on the pupils' achievement.

Secondly, the teacher must be able to recognize his or her own learning styles and be able to adapt these if necessary as appropriate. A teacher who is routinely stuck in the stereotypical 'chalk and talk' method of teaching will not achieve as much as a teacher who takes an active approach to teaching and learning and is willing to experiment with new teaching styles, methods and ideas.

There is a marked difference between talking *to* and talking *at* a class. When a teacher talks *to* the class they are also listening to their students, recognizing and accepting their opinions and allowing them to fully participate in the lesson. I have, unfortunately, seen firsthand evidence of teachers talking *at* the class, being in total control and allowing little or no opportunities for the students to interact with the teacher or each other. All children, regardless of their academic ability, will subconsciously 'switch off' if they are forced to listen to too much information for too long. Guided learning positively improves pupils' standards of work and development. In instances where students are allowed to explore and pursue their own learning, their attitude shows a marked difference to when they are 'spoonfed' facts and information.

All humans will begin to lose concentration at different levels and ages, but it is reasonable to assume that if a task is uninteresting or does not motivate us in any way, we will lose concentration. An average secondary school student will be able to concentrate for a solid 20 minutes on one task. A child with an attention deficit will only concentrate on average for four to six minutes. Usual teaching practice indicates that 10 to 20 minutes on one subject is usually enough before the risk of losing some students' attention may present itself.

Children's physical and emotional being affects how they learn and is part of their learning style. For many children, learning is strongly linked to how well they achieve. Many gifted children enjoy learning new and difficult material; it makes them feel accomplished. Other children strive for good grades because they want the approval of their teachers, parents or friends. When children are absorbed and interested in their learning, they will perform better than when the subject bores them, and this is just as true for adult learners also.

Self-esteem often dictates how confident a child is in his or her own learning. Without suitable encouragement children will often feel that they have failed in some way, or that their skills and achievements are not recognized. Without the guidance and praise of another human being, a child may become isolated and depressed, their social interaction skills reduced to alarming levels. In contrast, this praise must be fair, consistent and appropriate. Without realistic goals and targets, learning would become dull and non-stimulating. As professional educators and responsible adults, we must ensure all children reach their potential. We need to constantly and consistently encourage, support and provide to ensure every student performs to his or her best ability. At the same time we must create realistic and attainable goals for students to achieve.

Teaching and Learning in the Real World

Learning is often perceived as an individual concept, where the child will learn and grow at his or her own pace. However, children who come from the same geographical area will have shared similar environmental, cultural and social experiences and are likely to share ideas. Learning ability is often inherited from influential adults; when a child comes from an educated family he or she is likely to be encouraged to learn. Class issues often have an impact on the child. Although financial constraints do not always affect the child's emotional ability, lower social classes do appear to demonstrate lower academic ability. Gender issues due to nature and nurture can also affect the child's learning ability. Children need time and space to discover the world around them, and at the same time be given constructive guidance to hone their learning and ability.

In modern society, computer knowledge has assumed great importance in the work place, and schools can offer excellent opportunities to prepare and educate students in these skills. By encouraging ICT use in the classroom, boys can increase their language skills while doing something they perceive to be technical as opposed to creative. This is linked to the natural genetic pre-programming of boys who respond to active learning styles, and as they can use modern technology to increase their learning it is less likely that they will perceived it as being a feminized learning approach.

Children's learning styles also differ when they are high-versus-low academic achievers. Although gifted youngsters learn differently from each other, and underachievers have differing learning style patterns, gifted and underachieving students have significantly different learning styles and often do not perform well with the same methods. Teachers must be aware of not adhering to just one or two teaching styles. There are as many teaching styles as there are learning styles, and in order to get the most benefit out of both, the two must be compatible. As teachers we need to understand and accept these differences. We need to change our teaching methods to suit our pupils, not to suit us.

Teaching and learning are a cyclical process that is continually ongoing. Both teachers and learners share the roles in this process, with every individual involved in the application and understanding of teaching and learning procedures. Learning ability should be linked to but not synonymous with academic achievement. Where one child may fail in national exams, he or she may have considerable talents in other areas. A qualification is simply a statistic and a measure of how well that child performed on that particular day; it is not an accurate measurement of the child as a whole learner. Children are people, not statistics.

6 Assessment – Strategies for Raising Achievement

While boys' underachievement is a problem in many schools, making exams easier and reducing coursework will still not resolve the issue, as changes in previous years have shown. Boys who have no hope of ever being academics should not simply be brushed off as another statistic of the underachieving, but should be given the chance to raise their achievement in other areas, not necessarily academically.

Exam and test results are not, and perhaps, should not be, the only way of monitoring pupils' progress. Any good teacher knows that assessment should be formative – assessment for learning, and summative – assessment of learning.

Formative Assessment

Formative assessment happens continuously within a classroom environment. It involves both the teacher and student in a process of continual review and consideration regarding levels of progress. The student needs to know and understand not only what level they are at, and where they aim to be, but also what processes they must employ in order to get there.

During formative assessment the teacher will provide constructive and encouraging feedback, allowing the students to take some responsibility for their own learning. Formative assessment also enables the teacher to adjust lesson planning accordingly and be instantly aware of any potential problems or difficulties within the classroom.

Formative assessment may take the form of ipsative assessment, performed by the teacher. Ipsative assessment focuses upon how a person's performance and achievements can be compared with their earlier performances and achievements, with a view to determining whether any improvement has been made, or any 'added value' brought about.

Summative Assessment

Summative assessment is not only carried out by the subject teacher, but also by a board of external examiners in accordance with the National Curriculum. Summative assessment is made at the end of a unit, year or key stage, or when a pupil is about to leave the school. It is used to make accurate judgements regarding the pupil's performance in relation to standards set nationally. Summative assessment provides an overview of the pupil's attainment at the end of crucial stages in their education. It also provides some essential information, which can be used to monitor the performance of the whole school, not just specific pupils.

Summative assessment can be divided into two distinct assessment methods: normative- and criterion-based assessment. Normative assessment is concerned with national target ranges and local education authority guidelines. It assesses the progress of the student in relation to others. Such assessment may simply involve ranking the students, or may involve scaling their marks or grades so that they fall on a standard distribution of some sort. This generally applies to cross-school achievements and can compare local and national levels of attainment.

Criterion-based assessment, the most common kind of assessment, is centred on regulated examination groups (such as AQA, OCR and Edexcel), and is used in the assessment of nationally recognized qualifications. Such assessment generally involves determining whether the student can carry out specific tasks or activities, within a particular situation or context, set to a minimum standard. It is usually carried out on a 'pass/fail', or 'competent/not-yet-competent' basis. The results are conclusive and usually not open to review.

It is necessary to be aware at this point that formative and summative assessment are not mutually exclusive, and many findings will be implemented in both areas and stages of assessment.

Why is Assessment Important?

Although we know what kinds of assessment take place, why are these so important to raising and maintaining achievement? Formative assessment in particular can be seen to be an exceptional asset in order to maintain effective and high-quality teaching standards. Not only does assessment allow the teacher to see exactly how the student is progressing, it also allows them to see how effective their teaching methods are in practice, if reviewed as part of a process of target setting.

While it is necessary for each student to reach particular attainment targets as outlined by the National Curriculum and by the school itself, it is also important not to let assessment become the Holy Grail of the learning experience. Doing well in exams and achieving merits is good, but learning a broad range of skills will ensure a better overall cross-curriculum result, and a well-adjusted and intelligent student.

Formative assessment should be an effective part of lesson planning. It sounds obvious, but it is vital that the teacher plans a lesson in accordance with his or her students' abilities. A teacher's planning should provide opportunities for both the teacher and student to gain and implement information that could lead to progress and attainment of higher targets. Planning should be flexible enough that new ideas and skills can be easily incorporated, and so that the students understand the goals they are pursuing and how their work will ultimately be assessed.

59

The acronyms WALT and WILF which pertain to teaching and learning methods are especially important to teachers here, as they give the teacher an opportunity to explain to the students what is expected of them.

WALT – We Are Learning To... This gives the teacher a chance to explain what the lesson means to the student. Instead of simply learning by rote, or learning 'dead' information, the student is clear about what the lesson is offering, and what skills or targets they can be expected to achieve.

WILF – What I'm Looking For... The teacher can fully explain to the student the levels of assessment and what kind of skills he or she will be looking for during the assessment process. It gives the student a fairer chance of actually achieving what they are supposed to. Instead of simply learning 'blind', the student can gain useful feedback and a clear idea of why they are being asked to do the task.

It is essential that assessment for learning is central to classroom practice. Much of what teachers do already can be seen as forms of assessment. Tasks and challenges are set as part of the curriculum subject where students are required to demonstrate their knowledge, their skills and their understanding. The teacher observes and judges, and decisions can be taken to improve or maintain learning strategies.

A whole-school involvement in all areas of the curriculum is also very important for assessment to work effectively. For example, in classes such as English, students are assessed not just in timetabled English classes, but also across the curriculum in all subjects where they are required to read, write, listen or speak effectively as the subject demands. Subsequently, the English teacher not only teaches his or her subject, but also provides a strong backbone for the rest of the curriculum subjects. A strong aptitude in English generally suggests a good all-round learner, who will achieve high standards across the curriculum with ease.

Another very important aspect of assessment is that of self-assessment. Students often work best when they work together and learn within a group. Interpersonal learning has been recognized as an exceptional learning strategy as each pupil learns from their peers and becomes responsible for their own learning. As well as improving social skills such as politeness and acceptance, learning within a peer group allows the students to gauge how other students are doing and at the same time learn from each other.

Peer assessment can be particularly useful in demonstrating to the individual exactly what is expected of them. Old-fashioned teaching methods, which were almost completely individual orientated, often relied heavily on copying and regurgitating work set by the teacher. In some subjects students simply copied from a textbook or the blackboard, leaving no real scope for the creative aspects surrounding the subject. Thankfully, modern-day teaching methods involve the students and allow them to consider key points both independently and as part of the class.

When students become more aware of their own learning, they begin to see the areas in which they need to develop and improve. In this way the student takes responsibility for his or her own assessment and can demonstrate skills and weaknesses without feeling intimidated. When pupils are involved in their own learning they understand their targets better than if they are simply following orders. They are also more interested in learning, because they actually want to learn.

Putting Assessment to Good Use in the Classroom

How can we put these assessment strategies to good use? Since I am an English teacher, I will use English and literacy skills as an example.

Secondary English is concerned with four key areas: Reading, Writing, Speaking and Listening. These are all very active learning criteria, and in many cases one exercise will be enough to monitor a student's progress in all four fields. When studying a set text the pupil can be involved in reading aloud with the class and teacher, which improves speaking and listening skills; they can be asked to continue reading the text individually to improve their reading and comprehension skills, and can be asked to write a review of the text, thus exercising their writing skills.

Strategies for Raising Achievement

This very simple process of events can be continued across the key stages and throughout the school; the teacher can then assess the student's ability across a variety of differing levels. As the student reads aloud the teacher can assess their speaking abilities and see if the student has gained confidence or finds some areas difficult. Through the written task the teacher can assess grasp of grammar, structure, spelling and understanding of the text. The entirety of the assessment should be kept sensitive and constructive.

Any form of assessment has some emotional impact for the student, and teachers must be aware of the impact their assessment strategies can have on the confidence and enthusiasm of their pupils. They should be as constructive as possible in the feedback that they give. Comments that focus on the work rather than the person are more constructive for both learning and motivation.

A good practice while marking work is to divide the feedback comments into three parts, where two parts are focused upon constructive advice and the third is a phrase of encouragement.

Teachers should give praise when it is deserved and never be derisory in their assessment. All assessments should be fair and appropriate, it does not do to give one student constant praise even if they are a star pupil!

A lot of teaching relies on interaction between student and teacher, and as subjects such as English focus on methods of communication, the student can expect to improve skills through everyday use as well as structured lessons.

Useful indications for student assessment in a core subject such as English can include:

♦ The level of communication used by the student – how advanced is their vocabulary and how do they implement this in their written work?

♦ How often does the student read for enjoyment and at what level is their reading in terms of curriculum expectations – when asked to choose a book for reading, what kind of genre or medium do they prefer?

♦ How well does the student read aloud; do they tackle complicated words confidently or still struggle with simple lexical structures?

♦ What kind of maturity and understanding of English does the student's writing show, do they write fluently or with difficulty, do they appear confident enough to tackle alien concepts or still need careful observation and guidance?

These are just a very small amount of formative and summative assessment ideas, which should be a natural part of teaching, as it is essential that the teacher listens and responds to his or her class as well as obeying National Curriculum structures.

Careful and constructive use of assessment will

undoubtedly improve students' achievement levels. Where clear goals are set and targets are realistic, the student can then see what is expected of them both as a learner and as an individual. Learning is not just about what you know, it is also about how you use that knowledge, and when assessment is proactive, higher levels of achievement will follow.

Key Strategies for Raising Achievement in the Classroom

Raising achievement has become a serious issue in schools, especially where boys are achieving signifi-cantly poor results in comparison to girls.

Raising achievement is not a task for one individual to take on. To successfully and continuously raise levels of achievement the whole education community needs to be involved. The three main starting points for making changes to boys' education provision are:

1   Raising awareness of the broad spectrum of issues.
2   Taking a whole-school, active approach to making changes, formulating strategies and recognizing problem areas.
3   A proactive classroom technique to engage and motivate both genders.

We have seen that boys and girls learn differently and how this might explain why girls consistently outperform boys in a number of subjects. We have also seen how assessment strategies can help us determine problem areas and readjust our teaching styles to encourage better, more effective learning.

The following are some helpful ideas for an individual approach to raising achievement in the classroom.

Setting targets

Boys need proportionately more feedback than girls to remain motivated and on-task.

In lessons there needs to be a clear lesson objective which all students are aware of. Tasks need to be clear, organized and easily understood. There should be obvious and attainable goals to work towards.

Homework can assist in this process, encouraging the children to have a positive attitude to school and adopt effective work habits outside the school environment.

- Ensure your teaching is of a good standard and accessible to all students.

- Give frequent and short deadlines.

- Make goals realistic and achievable.

- Set clear, short-term, individual targets.

- Work with each student to create individual targets.

- Help increase each pupil's confidence.

Strategies for Raising Achievement

Using the four-part lesson plan

In Key Stage 3 the four-part lesson plan is a necessity. Effective use of starter, introduction, development and plenary will ensure that the lessons are broken up into manageable chunks and that the lesson objectives and outcomes can be accurately achieved.

This strategy is also very useful in Key Stage 4 and beyond. Remember that all children love games, even older children, and if learning is made interesting and fun then they will absorb far more information and be more attentive in class.

* Explain the four parts of the lesson to the class. This way they can see at a glance what goals they should be working towards.

* Always ensure the class knows what learning outcomes and objectives the lesson will cover. Again, a clear knowledge of what is expected of them means they have a better chance to achieve it.

* Develop fun, interactive learning resources. Flash cards, 'cut out and glue' worksheets and good use of an interactive white board will engage and interest students.

Challenge

Boys respond positively to challenges, group tasks, time-related assignments and quizzes. Due to the natural competitiveness of boys, tasks that require them to pit their skills against each other will be appealing to them. Always emphasize that the task is not about finding 'winners', but to achieve their own personal best.

Younger students will respond well to 'prizes' such as merits or the occasional sweet, but do not overuse such approaches. If you find you need to bribe your pupils to do well then you perhaps need to take a different look at your teaching style.

+ Keep challenges short term but with long-term goals in mind.

+ Deliver work in short, bite-sized chunks, and teach boys how to break things down for themselves and organize their time.

+ Boys are naturally competitive and will work best if there is an element of competition present.

+ Ensure that pupils know that they should be improving on their personal best.

+ Do not spoonfeed them information but set models and structures that they can use to create their own work.

Rewards and monitoring

As with setting challenges, establishing a clear goal will help boys see the short-term targets and become more eager to attain them. Be practical and fair with your reward system. Remember, even a 'well done' or 'good work' written on their work is a reward.

Give boys 'time off' from academic learning when possible. Using a short learning game in a plenary session to recap the work done in the lesson will help the class wind-down and ensure they remember what they have learned in the lesson.

- Give positive, personal feedback. Use the boy's name in written and verbal comments.

- Be positive and encouraging.

- Close marking is needed but excessive correction is not necessary.

- Return work quickly.

- Always praise and reward good achievement, effort and behaviour to increase motivation.

- Boys thrive on praise but try to give it privately rather than publicly to reduce the possible impact of peer alienation.

- Monitor both short- and long-term progress.

- Respond to any requests for further assistance but ensure the boy does the work himself.

- Ensure the student knows that you have an honest interest in his progress and achievement.

Managing Boys' Behaviour

Discipline

Good discipline and behaviour management are the foundations of excellent teaching and learning. All teachers know it is impossible to teach a lesson if the pupils are misbehaving or not listening. Remember that it is your classroom and you should have complete control of what happens within it.

Be firm and fair and always follow up bad behaviour. When meeting a new class for the first time it is sometimes helpful to spend a couple of lessons getting to know the pupils and establishing ground rules. A little time taken out of the beginning of the year will help a lot in the long term.

Don't be afraid to stop the class and let them know that their behaviour is not acceptable. Remember, always tell them that it is their behaviour you have a problem with, not them. If a strategy or lesson plan is not working how you want it to, it is perfectly acceptable to change direction and try a new approach.

- Set clear boundaries for behaviour and the standard of work.

- Ensure they know that it is their behaviour you are angry with, not them.

- Don't let them get away with it. Follow up issues of concern or failure to meet deadlines vigorously. Set clear consequences for failure to complete work on time.

Strategies for Raising Achievement

- Let it be known that you have high expectations for every single student in your class.

- Don't be afraid to challenge boys if they produce poor work.

- Do not give negative comments but rather concentrate on how the pupil may improve on his current standard of work.

- Be aware that many boys with behaviour issues may resent any confrontation but eventually they will realize it is in their best interests.

Challenging ethos

The idea that 'boys will be boys' does them a disservice. As much as possible, show boys that they do not have to fit in with cultural or sociological stereotypes and that they can be their own person. Be especially positive when discussing gender roles, race, religion and culture.

- Ensure boys experience a non-macho atmosphere where achievement and academic success is accepted and expected.

- Make a concerted effort to steer boys away from the 'laddish' and 'anti-swot' culture that often inhibits their learning.

- Give examples of how peer pressure can be hindering

their progress and encourage them to think for themselves rather than following the group.

Learning styles

Boys often have a very 'active' learning style where they learn best by seeing, hearing and doing. When planning learning resources, keep in mind that boys respond best to video, OHPs, small amounts of clear text, ICT and worksheets with illustrations.

- Break tasks into sections with a number of different activities. There is no point trying to overload them with a lot of text.

- Keep resources neat, interesting and colourful.

- Boys are much better at kinaesthetic, practical activities. Allow them to get involved with the lesson.

- Change the focus every 20 minutes to keep them engaged and motivated.

- Boys are good at thinking speculatively. Encourage them to think about, reflect on and return to their answers.

- Give boys a choice of work. 'Workshop' classes where boys can work through a variety of different tasks will motivate them and keep them on-task.

- Use ICT effectively. Give boys good access to computers and interactive learning.

Writing frames and literacy

Boys need a lot of encouragement to discuss their ideas for narrative writing. They are not often very good at creative writing that involves feelings.

Boys usually prefer factual writing but they do have a tendency to like fantasy, science fiction, monster or adventure stories which can be used to lead them into other genres and writing styles. Encourage independent and private reading to improve performance. Reading can be fact or fiction depending on their choice.

- Give boys writing structures and guidelines to help plan their work.
- Using models, OHP and ICT is a good way of getting boys involved.
- Remember that often boys do not write as much as girls. Allow for this and focus on quality not quantity.

Tutoring and pastoral support

PSHE, Citizenship and tutorial sessions are an essential part of the National Curriculum and through these studies boys can learn a lot about life skills. These classes also give teachers an excellent opportunity to get to know their students as people.

Children are always fascinated by the idea that teachers have personal lives and recounting positive personal experiences is a good way of encouraging communication between teachers and students. Do remember to keep it professional and don't give too much away about your private life!

- Give excellent pastoral support and take an interest in the boy as a person, not just as a student.
- Help raise confidence and self-esteem by talking and listening to the student.

Organizing the Classroom

Children often need to be organized differently depending on the subject or lesson content and teachers need to employ a variety of groupings. This has been proven to be a very effective strategy for managing behaviour.

To encourage planning, drafting or redrafting, it is often useful to pair a girl and a boy together. This strategy uses both boys' and girls' gender strengths and they can support each other's writing and give feedback.

- Sit classes boy–girl and try to keep only two students to a table when possible.
- Be wary of lower sets dominated by boys. Low self-esteem issues are common in lower sets and boys need to feel that they have something to work towards, not that they have been 'dumped' in a poor ability class.

Strategies for Raising Achievement

Role models

Gender stereotypes often come from experiences within the home, and the attitudes of parents have a significant impact on how boys and girls perceive themselves.

Boys from one-parent families often do not see their fathers very frequently and as a result may find that the majority of adults they interact with are female. This is reinforced at primary school where there are few male role models.

Gender roles should be removed as much as possible in the school. The deployment of staff often gives out powerful indicators of gender roles. Many subjects are very gender stereotyped. For example:

'Masculine' subjects include: Mathematics, Sciences, Technology, ICT, Physical Education.
'Feminine' subjects include: English, Art, Music, History, Geography, PSHE, Religious Education.

This only reinforces the stereotypical idea that men are practical while women are creative. Ensuring that boys have good access to teachers of both genders in a variety of subjects will help challenge any preconceived gender ideas they have of the education system.

- Give boys plenty of positive, male role models.

- Encourage parental involvement and support – especially that of fathers or other influential males.

Health and diet

Many students, especially from poorer families, do not eat very well or watch their diet. As a result they often eat a lot of fat and sugar, which can have a detrimental effect on their levels of concentration.

Consuming too much sugar causes a rise in blood sugar levels, giving a false 'high', but after this has worn off the individual will 'crash' and his or her performance will drop. This is especially important in children with ADHD who already have trouble controlling their energy and concentration levels.

Studies have shown that people who keep hydrated by drinking at least eight glasses of water a day are more focused, motivated and have higher energy levels than those who do not.

* Encourage boys to cut down on or eliminate fast food, sugar and caffeine. These stimulants have a negative impact on performance and behaviour, especially in pupils who have behavioural difficulties.

* Advocate drinking water regularly to keep hydrated. This will improve concentration and motivation.

7 Patterns of Behaviour and Behaviour Management Strategies

The key role – among the many roles – of all teachers is to provide his or her students with a good, sound education. Professional educators know that their main aim is to pass on knowledge and encourage the learning process, helping to ensure that each student reaches their maximum potential not only as a learner but also as a human being.

In an ideal world, teachers would be able to walk into a class and teach a successful lesson without any adverse incidents, and every single pupil in the class would be attentive, motivated and eager to learn. Maybe in this ideal world, pigs might grow wings and learn to fly!

Every teacher knows that teaching isn't just about passing on knowledge. There are as many pitfalls and challenges as there are achievements. While a teacher's aim is to ensure that all their students learn and grow, the realization of this goal is frequently thwarted by the actions and misbehaviour of some students.

Perhaps, as you read this, you are a PGCE student, tentatively feeling your way through the minefield of teacher training. Perhaps you are an experienced teacher with many years of classroom experience under your belt. Wherever you are in your teaching career, one thing is certain: at some point you will have experienced misbehaviour in your classroom.

Teachers are not superheroes, as much as we might try to be sometimes – we are normal people simply doing our jobs. We are not just teaching and learning machines – we have emotions, feelings, families, hopes and dreams. However, while in a classroom environment, there are standard practices and expected ways in which we must behave. We will all, at some point, come up against a student who does not behave in the way we want them to. It is important as teachers to recognize our emotional reaction to the behaviour of these students and respond accordingly.

Patterns of Behaviour

Children's misbehaviour can generally be divided into four main categories. These are:

1   Attention seeking.
2   Power seeking.
3   Revenge seeking.
4   Escape by withdrawal.

There may be many complex psychological factors and

reasons contributing to this behaviour, but it is necessary in the first instance to treat this 'symptomatically' and as a matter of course endeavour to determine the root of the problem.

Students should always be provided with one-to-one opportunities to discuss their behaviour and take responsibility for their actions. A proactive approach is more likely to succeed than simply punishing bad behaviour but in order for this to work effectively all parties must be willing and prepared to contribute.

Behaviour issues are not merely the responsibility of one teacher or department, but rather the whole school should seek to improve strategies, identify problem areas and address difficulties. The students themselves should be seen to have an active role in identifying and improving their behaviour, and ideally should be consulted before any decisions or changes are made. It is particularly important to stress that the behaviour is the responsibility of the individual, but not, however, to focus solely on the negative aspects of this.

Praise should be given as and when it is due, and good behaviour should be rewarded appropriately to emphasize that responsible, good behaviour will lead to positive consequences.

Attention Seeking

Of the four types of behaviour issues, the most common is that of attention seeking. Here the student will shout out, show off, 'stir up' or be physically offensive to other students or teachers, and generally distract the other members of the class. This behaviour is more commonly seen in boys simply due to the more boisterous nature common in young males, particularly in early adolescence.

The attention span of boys is significantly lower than that of girls and as a consequence leads to them becoming bored and restless easily. These students may also fidget or find it difficult to sit still. They may find it difficult to be quiet or patient for periods of time. They may exhibit classic signs of ADHD behaviour and will demand constant stimulation. Of course, not all attention-seeking behaviour is due to a special educational need, and even the brightest and most able students may 'play up' in some lessons.

This type of behaviour is extremely irritating to a teacher. It is also very easy to become overly annoyed by it, and students are very able to sense this. Any teacher who is suffering a 'bad day' will know that it seems that their students are deliberately trying to annoy them even more! Do not worry, your students have not suddenly gained the psychic ability to read your mind, it is simply a case that your mood will be picked up on by your class.

Emotions are highly infectious things; a calm and relaxed manner will be identified and 'rub off' on your class, thus everyone stays happy. An aggressive or aggravated manner will also be noticeable to your students and is likely to make them mirror your behaviour. Once a student is able to determine what kind of behaviour will annoy you the most, you can be sure they will become very proficient at it!

Not everyone has the patience of a saint, and it can be quite a test of character to not show annoyance at behaviour that at times is quite simply infuriating. During my most trying of classes, I have been known to set my jaw and count to ten in my head to avoid an angry explosion. If a student is displaying attention-seeking behaviour it is imperative that you do not give them negative attention. By shifting your focus, you can tactically ignore unwanted behaviour, a highly difficult task when James has taken to walloping Steven over the head with a ruler for the umpteenth time that lesson!

It is very important to curb your natural and instinctive responses and tailor your behaviour so that it will calm rather than aggravate your pupils. Instead of focusing on pupils' bad behaviour, you can keep alert to them being good and reward this. Establishing class rules at the earliest possible opportunity will provide clear guidelines for you and your students to follow.

In my introductory lessons with a new class I give every student an A5-sized printed sheet of my class rules and ensure they all glue this into their Student Planners. I also display an A3 version of these rules in a prominent place in the classroom so everyone can see it at quick glance. I learned very early on that taking the time to go over these rules meant far less hassle in the long run. It also means that if my classes are being particularly unruly I can ask them all to turn to our class rules and read them through.

By having class rules, students are clear about what kind of behaviour I expect from them, and giving them the guidelines in print reinforces this even more. There can be no denying what I may or may not have said in previous lessons if it is there in black and white at all times.

These rules are not just rules for my students, but for me too. They act as a promise or contract between my class and myself through which positive values are upheld and consistently affirmed. They show that there is a level of mutual respect present between us, and respect is an exceptionally important tool in controlling behaviour within a classroom.

However, if you do use class rules, make sure you stick to them rigidly! It is often very easy to start off strongly with an excellent set of class rules but find that three weeks into the term they are being ignored. If you expect your class to follow these rules, so must you.

Setting positive and realistic targets also shows pupils what they can achieve. Children quite often miss the 'bigger picture'. They do not consider the consequences of their actions on a long-term scale, and they very rarely pause to question the reasons behind their behaviour. Regardless of how it may feel to you, it is very rare that a student will take the time to concoct a devious plan to make your life a misery.

I am sure that every one of us can look back on our school days and remember certain teachers who we periodically wound up to breaking point. We did not seriously consider the implications of our behaviour, only that it was highly amusing to watch old Mr 'Wiggy' Williamson go a spectacular shade of purple-red when he exploded in anger. The news that Mr Williamson had later suffered a nervous breakdown did not hold much relevance for us until years later. It is only when we became teachers ourselves we truly began to appreciate how much Mr Williamson actually had to put up with. It certainly puts things in perspective for you as an individual and a teacher.

With regards to attention-seeking behaviour, however, Mr Williamson's first mistake was to let our behaviour annoy him to such an extreme level. His second mistake was to show us that it had. Although it may seem impossible at times, being a good behaviour manager is on a par with being a good poker player. I don't mean that you wager your life away in every class (although, admittedly, it can feel like that!), rather, you must attain and improve your 'poker face'. Think of yourself as a lion tamer facing a cage of hungry beasts. Imagine you are Barbara Woodhouse (whose TV programme years ago featured her powers at calming troublesome pets) on a mission to stop dear Rover mauling the postman, the milkman and the paperboy. Show no fear. Show no reactions. Let it appear to wash over you and do not take it personally. However, do not simply ignore it.

There are many ways of neutralizing attention-seeking misbehaviour, one of the most effective being a simple change of tone of voice and the statements you give. Do not focus on negative phrases; try to create positivism and clarity though clear, calm and direct statements. Rather than focus on the individual(s) causing the disruption, extend your commands to the whole class. The key here is not to alienate, nor make an example of, the disruptive student, but rather to play on his or her instinctual desires to be a part of the group.

For example, when Tommy Smith is incessantly shouting out and prodding his neighbour with his pen and pulling Jessica's hair, the expected reaction from the teacher would be: 'Tommy! Stop messing around and leave Jessica alone!' This puts focus on Tommy and Jessica and shows him that his behaviour has (a) been noticed and (b) provoked a reaction from you. Thus, his attention-seeking misbehaviour has been rewarded, while Jessica, who has done nothing wrong other than be an unwilling victim of Tommy's silliness, is also being made to feel at the focus of your attention, and as a consequence may be uncomfortable or embarrassed. (It is worth mentioning here that child psychologists have often attributed this kind of behaviour from males towards females as a way of showing them they are sexually interested in them, or, in more broad terms, they fancy them! Bear this in mind when dealing with this kind of behaviour, as the embarrassment factor is often very high.)

A far better response to the above kind of behaviour would be to note Tommy's actions and, should it be appropriate, address the whole class by demanding their full attention. For example: 'Everyone, focus on me now.' 'Class, put everything out of your hands and look at the front.' 'I would like everyone to be on-task in this lesson.' What would also work is to compliment the rest of the class on their good behaviour. For example: 'I would just like to say a big "well done" to this class, your attitude is particularly good today.'

Only you will know which approach is best, and which tactics to use based on your expectations of the class, but the emphasis is to constantly and consistently establish and promote a positive behavioural attitude for all.

To put it in a nut-shell:

Attention-seeking students shout, show off, stir up others, distract others and lack concentration.

If a student is attention seeking we do not give them negative attention.

Useful strategies are:

- tactically ignore secondary behaviour;
- when their behaviour is good, give them praise;
- set realistic targets so they know what they can achieve.

Power seeking

The second most common misbehaviour type is power seeking. Students may be argumentative, defiant and stubborn. They may bully others physically or verbally and may be deliberately confrontational in class with you or other students. The most simple of tasks or commands may become a power struggle, with the student purposefully aiming to see how far he or she can push you.

This behaviour is more difficult to manage than attention seeking. It can make us feel angry and defensive, and our gut reaction is to feel personally challenged. For example: Tommy is not settling down and getting on with his work, instead he is flicking small pieces of eraser around the classroom at other students. When approached and asked to stop, Tommy defiantly flicks another piece of eraser straight at you. The instinctual reaction here would be, 'Tommy! How dare you do that! Stop that right now! I'm giving you a detention!'

A better way to deal with this is to say: 'Tommy, you are well aware that what you are doing is not acceptable in my class. I want you to stop doing that and to concentrate on what you have been asked to do. At the end of the lesson you will tidy up the mess you have made in my classroom. If you stop now then you can avoid getting yourself in detention later.'

This is a bit more long-winded, but it leaves the child with no doubt about what you will put up with and what you expect. If Tommy then decides to continue with his misbehaviour he can expect to be punished, and the emphasis now rests on his own personal choice.

If a student is trying to dominate us, we must not confront them. Ignoring gut reactions once again, we must endeavour to turn the negative into a positive, being assertive but not aggressive. It is essential to establish yourself as the person in control of the classroom. While equality and respect are all essential parts of forming a healthy teaching relationship with your pupils, never let your class be in any doubt of who is the leader of the class.

As teachers, we can often find ourselves becoming intimidated by stronger pupils, and it is easy to let this intimidation become noticeable to the students. Your body language and facial expressions will tell your students a lot about how you are feeling, and it is essential to ensure this displays a positive attitude. Standing tall, maintaining eye contact and displaying an air of responsibility and composure are all very necessary while in the classroom. A teacher who shuffles into the room, appears unorganized and nervous will not gain much control over their class. Even when faced with the most terrifying of classes, always assert yourself.

A helpful tip for women, I have found, is to wear high heels and power suits! Approaching the class as you would an important business meeting automatically gives you the control and respect you need.

When dealing with power-seeking behaviour, using 'I' statements to promote a positive attitude can help to diffuse any negative reactions. Focus primarily on what you want the student to do, not what you don't want him or her to do. When a student is being disruptive, it is easy to give a negative command. For example: Tommy is constantly pulling faces at the other students and refusing to comply with the tasks set in the lesson. He is disruptive and rude to you, using inappropriate language and gestures. It is obvious that he is seeing how far he can push you before you 'snap'.

The instinctual reaction is to give a response based around his behaviour: 'Tommy, stop pulling faces', or 'Don't speak to me that way', but these commands merely focus on the inappropriate behaviour that you are trying to deviate from. 'I' based statements give a clear idea of your expectations without giving acknowledgement to the student's blatant power struggle. 'Tommy, I want you to concentrate on your work now', and 'Tommy, quieten down and focus on what we're doing', are far better statements as they give simple commands where the student is left in no doubt of what is expected of them.

Many students comment on how teachers ask them to do 'pointless' things, or merely order them about in class. Teachers can offer ownership of the lesson to the student by explaining why you want them to do something. When a child truly understands what is expected of them they will be more likely to accept the demands without consequence. Just like an adult, children need to see a reason behind their tasks, instead of merely feeling dominated by someone who has more power than them.

As with attention-seeking misbehaviour, praise is also very important in creating a good relationship with difficult students. Take time to actively look for situations where the student has performed well, be it their attitude or standard of work, and give them the praise and recognition they deserve.

Again, in a nutshell:

Power-seeking students will be argumentative, defiant, may bully others, may be stubborn.

This behaviour is more difficult to manage and we may become angry or feel personally challenged.

If a student is trying to dominate then we must not confront them.

Useful strategies are:

- ◆ be assertive but not aggressive or confrontational;
- ◆ use 'I' statements to focus on what you want them to do;
- ◆ give praise for good behaviour;
- ◆ give students the opportunity to take responsibility and ownership of their behaviour.

Revenge seeking

Occasionally in your teaching career you may come across a student who simply seems to be 'out to get you'. Their behaviour may be nasty, cruel, destructive or violent. They may be unresponsive and deliberately antagonistic both in and out of class situations. This behaviour, known as revenge seeking, makes us feel hurt and hostile.

Frequently this kind of behaviour is due to low self-esteem issues, and a student will try to compensate for their lack of esteem by building a defensive wall around themselves, taking every opportunity they can to devalue others in order to make themselves feel better. Boys are often confused and uncertain about growing up and becoming men. They are told they have to be caring, sensitive and believe in female equality, yet they are also taught to be tough and macho. Most boys truly believe that they should never cry, that showing weakness makes them less of a man.

As boys grow older, their inner conflict grows. They feel a lot of pressure to be a 'real' man and not be seen as a wimp. Frequently, when boys get older, they express false self-esteem to mask their feelings of weakness and vulnerability. Often this is through over-exaggerating conquests and their lack of emotions and tender feelings. Adolescent boys in particular are likely to have much lower self-esteem than younger boys or of girls of the same age. To deflect these issues a boy will often try to make himself seem 'hard', or put others down to try to express himself as a dominant male. Many males who bully other children often have some very deep-rooted self-esteem issues.

In order to develop a good relationship with these students it is necessary to distance yourself from what they do, and try not to take it personally. It is very rare that a student will target you specifically as a person, but merely as a figure of authority. Although these may be the most difficult of students to deal with, a positive relationship is a necessity to breaking down the issues the student harbours.

Behaviour Management Strategies

As with all behaviour management strategies, the key aim when dealing with these kinds of students is to consistently emphasize positive behaviour. While it may seem almost impossible to reason with these students, merely chastising them for their actions is not going to reinforce positive issues with them. As a figure of authority it is important to set behaviour by example. Reacting defensively or aggressively will not have any impact on this student as they will merely see their own behaviour mirrored in you, and will then continue to act in this way, assuming that their behaviour is justified.

Power struggles between teacher and student are to be avoided at all costs; an 'eye for an eye' reaction will only serve to make the student's behaviour more aggressive to yourself and other students. Instead, it is more practical and usually more effective to initiate a reasoning process where showing the student the positive rewards of good behaviour may hopefully initiate a positive and calm response. The aim here is to show that if you are nice to me, I'll be nice to you, which in turn will create a good working relationship. For example: Tommy has come into your class obviously in a bad mood. You know he has been in trouble with another teacher that day and he hasn't got over that yet. When you ask him to sit down quietly he responds with an expletive and kicks his chair. Rather than take offence at his reaction or reprimand him instantly for his bad language, it is important not to escalate his bad mood. What would be good to say here is: 'Tommy, I want you to take a few deep breaths and try to calm down. When you are calm we will talk together about what is bothering you.'

Sometimes, a revenge-seeking student will push the boundaries so far that even reason will not reach them. Again, reacting aggressively will not prove effective, and it is more productive to grant the student a 'time-out' where they can calm themselves down and reflect on their actions. We are all familiar with the image of a naughty student standing outside in the corridor, or outside the headmaster's office, but while this is generally seen as a punishment, it also acts as a way of allowing the student to withdraw from the situation and reassess things in their own mind. For example: Tommy's attitude and bad mood has got worse through the lesson. He is shouting out inappropriately and using bad language towards you and other students when asked to get on with his work. He starts a verbal fight with another student and you realize that at this point you need to make some serious form of intervention.

Try to get as close to Tommy as possible while not invading his personal space. Ensure you are between him and the other student so that to continue with their argument they would have to shout around or over you. In a calm tone you would ask Tommy to leave the classroom. Do not simply order him out; rather, say to him: 'Tommy, your behaviour is disrupting my lesson and other students. I would like you to take a "time-out" for five minutes. Please go and stand outside this classroom until I ask you to return.'

As a teacher, the main benefit for you is that you

remove the problem from the classroom for a while and approach the issue later when emotions are (usually) not so highly strung. After all, the whole reason you are in the classroom in the first place is to teach; it would be impractical and potentially damaging to persist in pushing for a solution when a student is obviously not in a cooperative mood!

A 'time-out' can be as little as two minutes, rising up to the entirety of the lesson if need be, but be careful. The object of a successful educational environment is to include the students in the system. Excluding a student from your class also means that you are excluding them from their right to an education. It would be preferable to attempt to work around the problem rather than simply removing the cause.

As a lot of revenge seeking is due to low self-esteem issues, the student may be used to being cast aside and not listened to, or perhaps even being devalued by others. In my experience, sometimes even the 'nastiest', (and I use that word loosely) kids can be the most reasonable when approached correctly.

When dealing with this kind of behaviour, structure and set ground rules will be your saving grace. Ensure that all students are aware of your rules, and that everyone sticks to them rigidly. It is all too easy to simply shout at a student and demand they leave the room, but this should be used as a last ditch solution. Setting a system that clearly establishes the boundaries will be indispensable to you, the teacher, and to the student who then knows how far they can 'push' in your classroom. Keep these rules non-negotiable, and don't keep changing the goalposts depending on the student.

Sometimes teachers find it all too easy to be harsher on well-known troublemakers, but are a little more lenient on those who are not known to cause problems. When dealing with behaviour problems, your own feelings should not be an issue. Again, this reinforces the idea of being able to distance yourself from the behaviour and makes sure you do not take it personally, however hard that may be at the time!

In a nut-shell:

Revenge-seeking students can be nasty, cruel, destructive and sometimes violent.

If a student tries to devalue or intimidate the group through revenge-seeking tactics we must remain calm and react logically rather than simply punishing the student.

Useful strategies are:

- ◆ develop a good relationship with the student;
- ◆ put strong emphasis on positive behaviour;
- ◆ emotionally distance yourself from what they do and do not take it personally;
- ◆ give students 'time out' if necessary.

Escape by withdrawal

Some students really do not enjoy school at all. They find it a struggle juggling the demands of life and education. Interacting socially may be a huge challenge for them; perhaps they are not 'popular' or may be experiencing bullying or a severe lack of self-esteem. Some students merely find school pointless and boring and would rather not be there. There are hundreds of reasons why a student may try to escape by withdrawal, but in most cases the student feels stupid or hopeless, that they have failed in some way, and will frequently simply give up.

As teachers we must remember that it is sometimes very hard for students to see the 'bigger picture' that education shows us, as adults. They do not fully comprehend the implications that being successful, or less so, in school may have on their employment prospects in later life. They are constantly told that it is worthwhile to get good SAT results and good GSCE results, but many do not understand why.

Cast your memory back to being 14 and choosing your GCSE or O-Level subjects. Your thoughts are filled with television, football, pop or movie stars – you are not too concerned with what career path you want to follow and how you will pay the mortgage or feed the family. As adults, we accept these responsibilities as a part of growing up, but as a child you still expect to be taken care of and have no immediate financial or employment concerns. However, most children do still have some aspirations and dreams, and when failure looms on the horizon for them their instinct often is to withdraw and attempt to escape.

The 'lazy' student who does no work in class, but

prefers to spend their time daydreaming looking out of the window or doodling in their book, is perhaps not lazy at all. It may be that the work is not challenging them enough or is challenging them too much. Sometimes the threat of failure is so strong that these children actually set themselves up to fail by their behaviour. They convince themselves that there is absolutely no way they can succeed and therefore see no point in trying.

Sometimes it works the other way around. The fear of failing is so great that the child may set themselves up for failure by not trying so as to distance themselves from their failure. This is often employed as a vital defence mechanism, and the student will apportion blame elsewhere. The student may claim that they did not get enough help, or that the lesson was too difficult to understand. This in turn, leaves the student's feelings relatively unscathed. These are the students who frequently say 'It's too hard, Miss', or 'I can't do it'. While you will probably find yourself becoming very frustrated by this behaviour, never forget that the student is probably feeling even more frustrated.

If a student is trying to escape by withdrawal we must not do it for him or her. Forget the 'must try harder's, think more of 'never give up'. Sometimes it is all about taking it slowly and making baby-step progress. An old saying I find particularly useful here is: 'With perseverance the snail reached the Ark'.

To combat their withdrawal the teacher must work with the child to realistically plan strategies and targets for success. All achievement, regardless of how small and insignificant it may seem, should be acknowledged and praised. Set work should be broken up into 'bite-size' chunks, which are more manageable for the student.

'Differentiation' has become something of a buzz-word in education, but the benefits of differentiating your material to suit specific students in your class are enormous. Differentiation allows all the students to work towards one aim or objective in many different ways. It also improves the pace of learning, as they do not have to sit and struggle with their work, or wait for their peers to catch up; they can work at their own pace to their own academic level. Remember, just because you have 30 students in your Set Five class, this does not mean that all the students will be at the same Set Five academic level.

When students attempt to withdraw and exclude themselves from the learning process it is our job as teachers to bring them back and include them again. Working to clear targets, where achievement actually seems feasible, will encourage the student to take more interest in their work and work towards the goals set for each one of them. I have found it useful to tell a few white lies sometimes when dealing with this kind of student. While working to improve self-esteem, I have told students that they have been given 'special' work to do, shifting the focus onto the positive, rather than implying that the student is not capable or is in some way a lesser student academically. For example: Tommy has not been doing well in his studies of late and has become a dreamer in class. He is struggling to produce more than a few sentences each lesson and it is obvious that he has given up. Instead of getting on with his work, Tommy simply sits in class and doodles in lesson. Punishing Tommy in this case will only bring about more hostility towards you and the subject.

Rather than make Tommy struggle through something he obviously cannot do, set him the same kind of work but perhaps of a different level. For example, if students have been asked to write a descriptive piece of writing focusing on the use of adjectives and adverbs, give Tommy a pre-written piece where he only has to add the describing words. Tell him this is special work that you think he will be really good at, but do not draw attention to the fact that he has been given something different to the rest of the class.

Students who withdraw often just need to find a little bit of faith in themselves. If we can help them to find that, then we can bring them out of their withdrawal.

In a nut-shell:

Students who escape by withdrawal: feel stupid and hopeless and will give up.

If a student is trying to give up through withdrawal we must not give up with them.

Useful strategies are:

- set realistic, attainable targets;
- create plans for success that students can work to and by which they can actively see their own achievement;

◆ acknowledge all levels of achievement no matter how small;

◆ differentiate lesson plans to promote inclusion of all students in the class.

Violent behaviour

Although this is not a specific behaviour type, it is well worth mentioning in this section. Violent behaviour is often a subset of revenge seeking, and is probably by far the hardest to deal with. All teachers are aware of the potential risks of violent behaviour, especially those who work in so-called 'rough' schools, but all hope they are never confronted by it. From a legal stand-point, the only real rule is to ensure you keep yourself safe. Always be very careful when dealing with violent or potentially violent, confrontational behaviour.

While some members of society used to have 'love' and 'hate' tattooed on their knuckles, it now seems that every parent has an invisible 'negligence' and 'compen-sation' tattooed on theirs. Teachers do not just have a duty to provide education; they are also looked upon as positive and influential role models, and as such are looked upon to set examples of behaviour, while rein-forcing positive, social, moral and ethical ideals. So what happens when a teacher is called upon to deal with violent behaviour?

As with all types of behaviour management, and I am aware that I am repeating myself here, don't take it personally. Once you let your own personal emotions cloud your judgement then mistakes will surely be made. Whether the violence is directed at you or at another student, always remain calm. I will be the first to admit that this is not at all easy when faced with two, brawling, six-foot, Year 11 boys, but keeping a level head will mean you are better equipped at dealing with the situation.

The first thing to assess when dealing with violent behaviour is: what are the immediate dangers? These apply to you, to the students involved and to any other people who may be directly or indirectly affected. Your duty as a teacher is to uphold and maintain the welfare of your students, and in this case any decisions you make are crucial. Most schools have a policy in place which dictates the correct procedure in dealing with violent behaviour, but essentially it is for you personally to decide whether you should get involved.

If you are a strapping, six-foot-four, male PE teacher, you are probably going to be less fazed about breaking up a fight than a five-foot-two, timid, female, languages teacher. I apologize for the stereotyping here, but it is my experience that when it comes to violence in schools male teachers are far better equipped at dealing with it, especially if the aggressor is a male student. It is perfectly acceptable to decide not to intervene and to allow other teachers to deal with the issue.

If you perceive the situation to be too dangerous or too complex to deal with on your own, get back-up. And while I am on the subject of back-up, I cannot stress how important it is to become a member of a teachers' union. Just as you wouldn't drive a car without insurance, don't go into a classroom without union membership; although it is a very slim chance, it is just possible it could save your career if ever you find yourself in a sticky situation.

The second thing to assess is the people involved. When two children fight, it is usually the case that one child is the 'victim' in the situation and does not really want to be fighting. If it is possible to determine who is the aggressor in the situation, the best course of action is to remove the victim. Just like the saying, 'it takes two to tango', it also takes two to have a fight. When you remove one, the other has no-one to fight with. In situations in a classroom or playground environment, it is likely that other students will be around. Quite often these students will be the ones standing in a circle shouting 'Fight! Fight!', and finding the whole thing quite intriguing.

Remember, your duty is to provide care for all your students, make sure any bystanders are removed from the area and to avoid becoming part of the situation itself. If the violence is directed at you personally, then it is up to you which tactic you wish to take: fight or flight. Obviously, the first isn't an appropriate stance to take. What I mean by 'fight' is whether you decide to stand your ground and try to reason with the student and calm him or her down, or whether you decide to take 'flight' and get yourself out of the situation immediately.

During my PGCE year I was constantly reminded not to

get into a confrontational situation with any of my students, but at the same time I was very conscious of the fact that I may be 'losing face' with them. This harks back to one of my earlier points of being assertive, not aggressive. Non-violent intervention strategies must be implemented when dealing with this kind of behaviour. If this means you have to back down from a situation, so be it.

Whatever the situation, and however you feel about it personally, having students lose a little bit of respect for you and bearing the brunt of a few student jokes for a while is certainly far better than sporting a black eye or being the centre of a disciplinary investigation. I realize that the latter sounds extreme, but cast your mind back to any possible confrontational experience you may have had, and consider the worst-case scenario. However much you may think 'that will never happen to me', it does still happen, and in cases of violent students, it is far better to be safe than sorry.

The following is a useful checklist should you be faced with violent behaviour:

- Establish whether you feel safe with the student. If you feel unsafe, remove yourself from the situation immediately and call another teacher or member of staff to support you.

- Place yourself as close as possible to an available exit. If the classroom door is closed, attempt to open it if possible. Never get yourself in a one-to-one situation in a closed room. Where possible, call for another member of staff to be with you or send another student to summon someone.

+ Stay calm and attempt to gain control of the situation by clearly addressing the issue of concern. Show that you understand the student's distress and are attempting to deal with the issue.

+ Clearly and directly explain the kind of behaviour that is acceptable and unacceptable. If the student is shouting, ask them to lower their voice and try to calm down. Never shout back at the student, it will only intensify the situation.

+ Be especially careful with body language and personal space issues, do not touch the student or crowd their personal space. Be aware of your movements and do not make any sudden or potentially threatening motions, which the student may misinterpret.

+ Never grab, push or slap the student. If the student physically attacks you, always attempt to protect yourself but do not retaliate in a violent manner towards the student.

+ Do not threaten, taunt or back a student into a corner, and do not allow yourself to be backed into a corner. Always stay in an open area, preferably with an object such as a table separating you both.

+ Always remember to write an incident report as soon as possible after the event and ensure the correct authorities both in and out of school are notified.

Managing Boys' Behaviour

Violent behaviour is not as common as the media would have us believe. However, it does happen, and all teachers should be aware of how to deal with it, taking advice and undergoing training wherever possible. The last thing I want to do here is to scare any trainee teachers into believing that the classroom is a dangerous place. As with any job, there are always some dangers in the workplace. The key to being successful in any situation is in knowing how to deal with it and being prepared for the unexpected.

Unfortunately, misbehaviour rarely follows set rules and scenarios, and it is up to you as a teacher to assess how best to deal with the situation. By remaining calm and in control and using positive behaviour strategies, you can be sure that any behaviour incidents will improve as your experience grows.

Behaviour Management Checklist

To take a proactive approach to any behaviour issues, always stay 'SANE' (see the following):

Stop – Always ensure you stay calm, positive and in control. Always react in a professional manner. Never react hastily or aggressively.
Assess – Consider the situation and the pupils involved. Always be sure about what is happening before you decide to take any action. If pupils are in danger,

always remove them from the situation as soon and as safely as possible.

Negotiate – Talk to the student involved. Do not shout. Try to find out why they are behaving in this way and if they themselves can offer any solutions to the problem. Explain why their behaviour is unacceptable and show why the consequences are necessary. Always fit the punishment to the crime.

Evaluate – Ensure the situation has been resolved and take action to follow up any circumstances if necessary. Think about how the student reacted to you and if your response was accurate and effective. Learn from any mistakes in case this behaviour happens again.

Dos and Don'ts

Do

* Keep calm and professional at all times.

* Always ensure you are in control of the situation. Do not react instinctively, but take your time to react accordingly.

* Give the student the opportunity to take responsibility for their behaviour and change it accordingly.

* Ensure the student understands why their behaviour was wrong and explain the consequences. Set firm but fair punishments.

- Tactically ignore unwanted behaviour where possible – don't make mountains out of molehills.

- Make sure you know the school policy on discipline procedures, such as giving detentions or putting a child on report.

Don't

- Deal with a student when you are angry. Always take time to calm down.

- Punish a student unfairly or without real cause. Always ensure you are positive about what the student has done and make sure the punishment fits the crime.

- Physically touch the student. Never slap, push or grab a student under any circumstances.

- Punish the whole class when only one student is directly responsible.

- Remove the student from the classroom unless you really have to. Always ensure students who are removed from the room are supervised in some way.

- Bear grudges against individual students. Once the behaviour has been dealt with, start a clean slate.

Behaviour Management Strategies

Helpful tips

Tip 1 – Always establish with a child who is misbehaving that it is their behaviour that you dislike and not the child. Say it aloud to them: 'I am not happy with your behaviour and right now I am angry with that behaviour.'

Tip 2 – If an incident happens in class don't be afraid to send a child out for short periods or move them to another area of the room. Give it a label such as 'time out' or 'cool off time'. Always make sure that the child knows that you will give them time to explain that particular incident. Make a time that's convenient for both of you, even if it has to be the following day.

Tip 3 – Allow the student time to explain why *they* think they are behaving in such a way. If they find this difficult to do verbally, or find it hard to write things down, design an 'incident sheet' that will allow them to draw:

+ what happened;

+ why they reacted the way they did;

+ what alternative action they could have taken;

+ what they will do next time if this situation arises again.

Tip 4 – Circle time is a very effective way of finding out about your children and their interaction with others. This is one of the best ways of discovering how the class feel about each other and of finding ways to resolve any conflict. Encourage all children to speak in this forum. Start in a simple way and go around the circle. For example: 'I like Tommy because he is always helpful and polite in class.' Then go on to a statement such as: 'I hate being at school when ...' Then ask the class themselves to make suggestions. Keep circle time short, 20 minutes on a Friday afternoon is usually very helpful.

8 Special Educational Needs and Behaviour Management

Special Educational Needs, or SEN as they are more commonly known, cover a massive spectrum of possible difficulties or issues that students may face in the education system. A child is considered to have special educational needs if he or she has a learning difficulty that requires special educational provision to be made for them.

Although many children may have learning difficulties, a child will be added to a school's SEN register if the difficulty is seen to be significantly greater than the majority of other students of the same age. SEN children will be educated in mainstream schools provided that:

- They are being provided with the educational provision they need.

- Any provisions that need to be made do not interfere with the education of others.

• The resources and provisions needed are available within the school.

Just as every child is an individual, SEN children are just as different from each other as any other children. Even when a child is 'diagnosed' as having a particular special need, their needs may not be the same as another student with the same SEN.

The list of types of SEN is massive and many children may have difficulties in more than one area of learning. In order to break down the list of possible conditions, every SEN can be placed in one or more of the following three categories:

1   Learning Difficulties: the most common SEN, these can range from moderate (MLD) to severe (SLD) and may or may not be related to a physical or medical condition. Examples include dyslexia, dyscalculia and speech and language disorders.
2   Behaviour Difficulties: while no student is well-behaved all of the time, students with a behaviour difficulty will exhibit more pronounced behavioural issues. This may be caused by a physical or medical problem or a learning difficulty. Examples include Attention Deficit Hyperactivity Disorder, Autism Spectrum disorders and Tourettes Syndrome.
3   Physical and Medical Difficulties: there is a broad spectrum of these difficulties that may not always be physically obvious. Examples include hearing and sight impairments, mobility issues, cerebral

palsy and 'hidden' disabilities such as diabetes, epilepsy and asthma.

The number of male students with a SEN is more than double that of females. SEN students may be given a Statement by a professional specialist to determine the level of help the student may need. Studies conducted by the DfES estimate that 3 per cent of all pupils (approximately 250,000 children) in the UK have a special educational need and have a Statement. Sixty per cent of these pupils are educated in mainstream schools. A further 14 per cent of students are likely to have some form of SEN but do not have a Statement.

The *Excellence for all Children: Meeting Special Educational Needs* Green Paper (1997) and the Special Educational Needs and Disability Act (2001) meant that approaches to inclusion and special educational needs were reviewed and changed to ensure that all students have equal rights and access to education provision regardless of their circumstances. Schools are not merely a place to learn academically, but also to learn socially and discover essential facts about life in modern society. Inclusion ensures children are accepted and are treated equally, making them a part of society, not separating them from it.

All schools are now expected to devise a SEN and Inclusion policy that demonstrates their recognition of students with special needs, and the provisions they make for these students. Many schools work with Special Educational Needs Coordinators (SENCO) to assess the needs of particular students and to discuss the provisions and changes required to include the student in mainstream school education. The school and the SENCO decide on any action needed to help the student to progress in light of their assessment. Strategies will be formed and decided on to ensure that the student is being given the provision he or she needs.

These strategies work together to ensure that the student can remain in mainstream education and reduce the need for specialist schools. In addition to these, the school puts together Individual Education Plans (IEPs) to enable the student to progress. These IEPs include information regarding:

- the short-term targets set for or by the student;

- the teaching strategies used;

- the provision to be put in place;

- when the plan is to be reviewed;

- outcomes to be recorded when the IEP is reviewed.

The IEP only records areas that are additional to or different from the differentiated curriculum provision and focuses upon three or four areas to match the student's needs. IEPs are reviewed at least twice a year and parental views are sought on their child's progress. The student is also invited to contribute to the review process and be actively involved in setting the targets.

Dealing with Behaviour Problems in SEN Pupils

Behaviour issues are not limited to SEN pupils, but dealing with their behaviour can be more complicated than dealing with children without an SEN.

The list of possible special educational needs a pupil may have is huge. The following explanations and teaching tips cover the six most common SEN and behaviour problems in boys. The tips and strategies are not exclusive to SEN issues or difficulties and can be implemented when dealing with the behaviour of any student.

I have included an in-depth review of ADHD/ADD, as recent reports and studies show that instances of this particular SEN are highly prominent in young boys with behavioural problems.

Emotionally Disturbed or Behaviourally Challenged Pupils

- Boys are four times more likely than girls to be behaviourally challenged.

- This kind of behaviour is likely to differ from day to day.

- Children may fluctuate from being withdrawn and hostile to friendly and sociable.

- They may have difficulty controlling their emotions and frequently have aggressive outbursts, often bullying others.

+ They may have problems accepting authority and will openly challenge other individuals to get their own way or to get attention.

+ They will have very low self-esteem and be unable to take a joke. They are likely to feel continually criticized and blamed.

+ They will frequently exhibit bad behaviour such as: swearing, shouting out, disobeying commands, demanding immediate attention, purposefully trying to annoy others and damaging property.

Teaching tips
1 Always praise and reward good behaviour and progress. If possible ignore the bad behaviour.
2 Try to avoid situations where the child may get angry. Always say something positive and try to keep the child calm.
3 Always show that you understand why he feels angry and offer alternative ways that he can express this. Allow the child to come up with his own strategies to take responsibility of his behaviour.
4 Be open, assertive and helpful but do not pander to the child.
5 Have a good sense of humour and try to ease tension with a joke. Never use sarcasm as the child will not understand it.
6 If necessary, give the child an 'exit plan' so he can have a time out to calm down. Sending him on an

errand or letting him give out books can help him redirect his attention and reduce his anger.

Autistic Spectrum Disorders

Autism is a medical condition involving a range of conditions that affect the way a child may communicate or relate to another person. Autism can occur at a variety of levels from mild to severe learning difficulties.

◆ The child may have an obvious lack of social skills and empathy for others, often being seen to be in a 'world of his own'.

◆ The child will dislike change and will prefer routines. Changes to routines may upset and confuse the child.

◆ He may become particularly obsessed with one subject and show exceptional skills in this.

◆ The child may show an inability to express himself and have a poor command of language.

◆ He may frequently indulge in repetitive behaviour such as rocking, making noises or repeated physical movements.

Teaching tips
1   Always tell the child what should be done rather than what shouldn't be done. Keep commands short, simple and to the point.

2   Use visual aids to help explain work or to signify what you would like the child to do.
3   Do not use sarcasm or idiom. The child will not understand and will take what you say literally.
4   Encourage interaction and allow the child to try and express himself in his own way.

Asperger's syndrome

Part of the autistic spectrum. Children usually exhibit many of the same tendencies as those with autism, but tend to be more sociable and well mannered with a good sense of humour.

♦ The child may dislike working in groups and lack creativity and imagination.

♦ He may make repeated motor movements or have specific rituals or routines. He may be obsessed with certain areas of a task or subject.

♦ He may try to interact with others but will do so in an inappropriate or naive way.

Teaching tips
1   Provide structure and order for the child and always concentrate on simple, positive commands. Praise and reward good behaviour and progress.
2   Keep instructions simple and to the point. Always ensure the child is giving you his full attention

and ensure he understands what you want him to do.

3   Don't be ambiguous when explaining things to the child. Words such as 'naughty' and 'silly' do not mean anything to the child.

4   Encourage calm, cooperative behaviour and allow the child to socialize if he wants to. Explain the importance of interaction and empathy towards others.

Dyspraxia

This can vary from being mild to severe. It may affect speech and will cause motor problems.

• The child will have a very low self-esteem and possible mental or anxiety problems later in life.

• This condition affects physical movement and organization. It may also affect academic learning and life skills.

• The child will have problems coping with multisensory stimuli and may feel pain or discomfort from being given too much visual or aural information all at once.

• The child may have literacy difficulties and may appear clumsy and disorganized, however he will have good verbal skills.

• He may lack in concentration and motivation and often appear lazy or distracted.

117

Teaching tips

1   Seat the child away from any distractions such as doors and windows and ensure he is close enough to see and hear you properly. Ensure he sits upright with both feet on the floor.

2   Break tasks down into 'bite-size' chunks to make the work more manageable.

3   Keep spoken instructions clear and to the point. Repeat them if necessary, and get the child to repeat them back to you to ensure he has understood.

4   Use sheets with spaces for answers to reduce writing space. Use lined paper attached to the desk so the child does not have to hold it as he writes.

5   Use mnemonics to assist spelling and short-term memory. For example:

     I before E except after C

     Because: Big Elephants Can Always Understand Small Elephants

     Necessary: 1 coffee (C) 2 sugars (S)

     The order of the planets in distance from the sun: My Very Easy Method, Just Set Up Nine Planets (Mercury, Venus, Earth, Mars, Jupiter, Saturn, Uranus, Pluto)

Specific literacy difficulties – dyslexia

Boys are three times more likely to be affected by dyslexia than girls. There are three main types: visual, auditory and motor.

118

* Dyslexia causes significant problems with reading, writing and spelling, and in some cases, numeracy.

* The child will find it difficult to read aloud or may take a long time reading even short passages.

* The child may have poor short-term memory and problems distinguishing between right and left.

* He may often write letters and numbers the wrong way round or in the wrong order.

* He may be particularly bright in other areas, with an aptitude in creativity.

* Frustration and a lack of self-esteem may be obvious.

Teaching tips
1   Always focus on what has been done and give praise and encouragement for progress made.
2   Do not overload the child with too much information at once and give them extra time to complete a task if possible.
3   Where possible use visual aids to assist the child, and encourage the use of ICT, diagrams, etc.
4   Give the child a personal word bank and display keywords and vocabulary on the walls of the classroom to provide assistance.
5   Use frameworks to provide support and help the child gain a clear idea of what is expected of him.
6   When marking work, do not highlight all the mistakes or use too much red pen, as this will be

very daunting for any pupil. Where possible use a more 'friendly' colour and use simple symbols to show any mistakes.

Attention Deficit Hyperactivity Disorder/ Attention Deficit Disorder

Attention Deficit Hyperactivity Disorder (ADHD) and Attention Deficit Disorder (ADD) are genetically determined medical conditions, which affect the parts of the brain that control attention, concentration and impulses. They are three times more common in boys than in girls and are characterized by:

* restlessness;

* mood swings;

* poor concentration;

* disruptive, impulsive behaviour.

ADHD may be present in addition to other learning disabilities such as dyslexia, dyspraxia or difficulties with language tasks. Children who have significant problems in concentration and attention, without the overactivity, are often described as ADD rather than ADHD.

ADHD/ADD is usually first noticed in early childhood and is far more than just simple misbehaving. Scientists estimate that up to 7 per cent of school children are affected by this disorder in the UK. It is not a new concept or 'disease', elements of ADHD/ADD have always been present, but recent research into the disorders have not only given them a name, but have offered possible ways to treat it.

In the past, naughtiness, possible emotional problems, and even bad parenting have explained the symptoms of ADHD sufferers. The cases of ADHD are not increasing, but as more research is conducted into the affliction, more cases are being properly diagnosed and information is more widely available. ADHD/ADD is most commonly noticed in school age children from the age of five, and 80 per cent of those diagnosed with ADHD go on to exhibit symptoms into adolescence and 65 per cent continue to have symptoms during adulthood.

ADHD is a genetic disorder, and is therefore not caused by bad parenting. Research suggests that changes in the parts of the brain that control impulses and concentration may increase the likelihood of ADHD, and inherited, genetic and environmental factors may also contribute to the disorder. Due to its genetic link, if a family has one child with ADHD, there is an increased chance, up to 35 per cent, that another sibling will also have the disorder, and a 45 per cent chance that at least one parent will have this condition. In cases of identical twins, the likelihood that both children will have ADHD is approximately 90 per cent.

Some research has suggested that ADHD can also be

due to injury during foetal development to certain parts of the brain. Misuse of alcohol or tobacco during pregnancy, premature delivery and head injury after birth may all cause ADHD/ADD symptoms.

While social factors such as bad parenting, family disruptions or stress, excessive or prolonged viewing of visual media and diet may all have an aggravating affect on ADHD, they are not the cause of the condition.

There are four steps in treating ADHD sufferers:

1   An experienced and suitably qualified child psychiatrist or paediatrician properly diagnoses sufferers.
2   Parents and teachers are given relevant and useful information regarding the disorder.
3   Parents, teachers and professional healthcare staff discuss behavioural therapy and education support for the sufferer.
4   Sufferers may be prescribed medication to help with the symptoms.

It is widely accepted that all four of these steps are used when treating ADHD sufferers to ensure they get the best possible care and support to overcome their affliction.

Although most people with ADHD go on to lead very full and fulfilling lives with the proper care and support, a small number of sufferers find their disorder to be a real problem, which affects them from childhood into adulthood. The possible consequences of ADHD on a sufferer's life include:

* Poor performance and achievement in school, college and employment.

* Depression, anxiety and metal health issues.

* Poor relationships with others or inability to form meaningful relationships. Children may find it hard to share things or may frequently get into fights.

* Problems finding or keeping a job, or sufferers may exhibit poor behaviour while in an employment environment.

* Higher risk of exhibiting aggressive or antisocial behaviour.

Using drugs to control ADHD/ADD

When behavioural and emotional support is not enough to control the symptoms, some sufferers may be given stimulant medications that affect certain chemicals in the brain. These medications increase attention and reduce hyperactivity, and may be used to treat ADHD and hyperkinetic disorder.

The most widely used drug to treat ADHD in the UK is methylphenidate, or Ritalin as it is more commonly known. Ritalin stimulates the central nervous system and has earned the nickname 'kiddie coke', as the effects are similar to cocaine or amphetamine use in adults. The effects of the drug begin within 30 to 60 minutes and long-lasting forms can have an effect of up to 12 hours.

Medication may continue for several years, but it is recommended that the dose is greatly reduced if not stopped altogether after the onset of puberty, although some sufferers may need to continue the medication as adults. Common side-effects include reduced appetite and a reluctance to go to sleep. Anxiety, nervousness, nausea, headaches, dizziness, drowsiness, twitches and a tendency to be over-focused are also other possible side-effects. The long-term consequences of the drug are not yet known, although there are no known harmful effects from using this drug over several years.

Figures from 2003/2004 show that 250,000 prescriptions for Ritalin were dispensed by GPs. This is a huge rise from the early 1990s when only 2,000 prescriptions were dispensed. The cost on the health industry is rising in an attempt to calm Britain's hyperactive children. Ritalin abuse is also common, and girls may take the drug as a slimming aid to reduce their appetites.

Behaviour management for children with ADHD/ADD

For schools, ADHD is a rising problem. Some children are not properly diagnosed and so do not get the help they need. For others, their parents do not want to accept that something may be 'wrong' with their child and blame the school system or government for not providing satisfactory education. For a teacher faced with students with ADHD/ADD, lessons and behaviour management can be a real struggle.

As with all behaviour management, the focus needs to be on the child, not on how annoying, distracting or frustrating their behaviour is for a teacher. The following are some helpful tips and strategies on how to teach children with hyperactivity disorder.

Sitting still and giving instructions

- This is virtually impossible for children with ADHD/ ADD. Instead of being overly firm with him and forcing him to sit rigid in his seat, let him fidget or play with something *while* he's listening.

- An excellent strategy to reduce unwanted movement is to give the student a stress ball to play with. This gives him something to focus on kinaesthetically while listening to your instructions at the same time.

- Make sure you maintain eye contact and keep your instructions clear and precise, repeating yourself if necessary. Ask the child to repeat back to you what is required of him so there is no doubt that he knows what is expected of him.

- Let an ADHD student respond more orally, and take the emphasis off written work as much as possible. These children often struggle with linguistic-based learning and making an ADHD student do too much writing will only make them more frustrated, and as a consequence, more likely to 'play up'.

Avoiding distractions

* Distractions of some kind are inevitable in the classroom. There are a million and one things to look at and lots of other people around who are frequently making a noise or moving about.

* Sit the child as near as possible to your desk while still integrating him into the classroom. Visual displays should be informative and educational – after all, if he is going to stare around the room, at least this way he can absorb something useful!

* Music is also very useful, and can improve concentration in all students, not just ADHD sufferers. Using calming, non-intrusive auditory stimulation will help keep students focused.

* Movement is also very useful to integrate into the lesson, this helps with coordination and concentration and is a fun way to get all students involved.

* Using cards, beanbags, and hand signals are all ways to get students interested in a lesson while also improving their motor skills. ADHD students often do very well in drama as their natural enthusiasm and desire for movement can be put to good use.

Teaching style

◆ While an enthusiastic and upbeat teaching style is beneficial to motivate students, be careful you don't get *too* overexcited as this will only encourage the ADHD student to become overexcited as well! Try to keep your teaching style calm and clear, while still projecting your own enthusiasm for the subject.

◆ ADHD sufferers have trouble focusing and keeping on-task. Remain positive and maintain a well-structured lesson, going over certain points if you need to.

Discipline

◆ While ADHD sufferers have a problem with control and behaviour, being overly harsh will not solve any problems, indeed it is likely to make them worse. Similarly, not providing ample discipline will only cause you more problems in the long term.

◆ Ensure you have some pre-established consequences for misbehaviour that are equal and fair for all students. Make sure classroom rules are enforced consistently.

◆ Remain calm, give clear and concise instructions and avoid arguing with the student. If the student has a temper or becomes violent, do not argue with him but give him a time-out if necessary. Refuse to retaliate angrily, and keep calm and in control at all times. Informing the student just what you will and won't put up with in your class is essential so that all students know where they stand.

* Give warnings if necessary but administer discipline immediately and positively – make it clear that any form of misbehaviour will not be tolerated.

* Do not be overly critical or harsh when disciplining ADHD students. Remember, a lot of ADHD behaviour is not their fault and damaging their self-esteem will do far more harm than good. This is always worth remembering when dealing with any 'naughty' child. Discipline should be firm but fair. Being sarcastic or making overly critical comments will not only be unfair to the child, but will probably raise hostilities between you. It is also very likely to land you in hot water with your department if your attitude does not remain professional at all times!

* Ensure the punishment fits the crime. Often, ADHD sufferers are not quite sure what they have done wrong and may need guidance to ensure they understand the implications of their actions.

* If the ADHD student takes medication, avoid publicly reminding him to take it, and thus drawing attention to his affliction. Instead, monitor his behaviour closely and give one-to-one attention and reminders when necessary.

Encouragement and rewards

◆ ADHD students often need more encouragement and praise than other students. Always reward more than you punish and put the focus on how good behaviour gets good rewards.

◆ Building self-esteem is very important, and good behaviour should be praised and rewarded immediately. Encouragement and guidance will help the child to see you as an ally not an enemy, but ensure your rewards are accurate and change them if they do not seem to be working.

◆ Let the child talk positively about himself and ask him how he felt about achieving something successfully. Ensure that the child sees how well he is doing, as opposed to his failings.

◆ ADHD students do not need any 'special' treatment, but teachers do need to be aware of the potential problems that may arise. As with all SEN issues, awareness and understanding are the key focal points for success. There is no point wrapping a child in cotton wool or getting frustrated with his behaviour. It is important to understand his limitations but at the same time to encourage him to do the best he can. Giving him realistic and attainable targets will not only improve his self-esteem, but will make him realize just how much he is capable of.

Managing Boys' Behaviour

Schools can help greatly with ADHD students in many ways, providing them with a good basis on how to succeed in life. Key support strategies include:

1. Offering support and counselling if needed to help raise self-esteem, while also raising awareness and addressing any of the possible problems a student may face.
2. Assist with organization skills, reading and writing, maths and other core skills to ensure the student gets as much as possible out of school-based education.
3. Provide therapies if needed for speech, coordination and behaviour management and give good guidance on how to behave and achieve in school.

For a teacher, having a student with a SEN in the class does not automatically mean that that student will be a 'problem'. Knowing how to approach and guide the student is exactly the same as knowing how to deal with any student. Patience, understanding, acceptance and a positive outlook are all necessary when teaching children, and children with special educational needs are no exception.

9 Looking After Yourself

Successful teaching is hard work. Anyone who tells you otherwise has either been exceptionally lucky or is a complete liar. Teaching can be a great, satisfying and incredibly stimulating career, but it can also leave you feeling very drained, depressed and dispirited. When day after day you seem to be teaching kids who don't want to be there and don't want to learn, the enjoyment factor in teaching can get lower and lower.

It is on days like these that I reach for my trusty teaching diary, flip to the front page, and remind myself yet again why I wanted to be a teacher. I often find that soaking in the bath with some bubbles and a nice glass of Australian red does wonders too!

But, what do you do when you become bogged down with behaviour management and none of your strategies seem to be working? Believe me, I have been there, and so have most other teachers. Teaching isn't a one-man profession, it's teamwork, and as such every teacher needs to find guidance and support from their peers. Teachers who feel as if they are struggling on their own need to find a support network to help them.

Stress is widely recognized in the teaching profession as being the number one cause for illness and for leaving the profession. It is easy to understand why when you consider the workload and pressures put on teachers. Not only do we have to deliver satisfactory to excellent lessons, ensure our students are motivated and well behaved, cope with planning, marking and finding resources, we are expected to be professional at all times and keep a big grin on our faces even when we can't find much to smile about.

Teaching is indeed a tough profession, but by bringing all your skills and experience into action you will soon find it is not all doom and gloom but a highly rewarding career

Do not let yourself become disheartened or bitter, but allow yourself some time to reassess things in your own mind. Always remember to switch off when you get home, and only do as much as you really have to do. There is no point letting teaching become your complete life and losing sight of who you are as a person. I have said it many times before, and I will say it once again, never take a student's behaviour personally.

The student who drives you up the wall with their bad behaviour and total hatred of the education system does not lie in bed thinking up devious ways of making your life hell. The student who never hands in homework and does as little as possible in class is not thinking to themselves, 'how can I wind up Miss today?' In some very small cases, yes, there are students who do this, but as a general rule, most students simply do not realize just how much of an impact their behaviour has on you as a teacher. I would take a bet that most of them would be absolutely mortified to find you crying your eyes out in the staff room because of something they had done in your class.

A good example of this is that when I left one particular school the one class that was the bane of my life (and the students who I quite cheerfully could have throttled on many an occasion!) took the time to make me a card, apologize for their behaviour, wish me well and beg me not to leave. When I put in perspective the tears I cried out of sheer frustration, and the tears I cried from being so incredibly touched by what they had done for me, there could be no denying that their actions reaffirmed why I chose to teach in the first place.

For many students, you as an individual are not the enemy, it is simply because you are a representative of the education system as a whole that you receive the brunt of their frustration and anger. Teaching is not just about sharing and projecting knowledge, it is also about having an honest and true desire to make kids' lives better. While managing behaviour and improving achievement is a constant battlefield in many schools, taking time out to get to know the kids and to give them the respect they deserve as people will make life for everyone, both the teachers and the students, much easier.

Ten Helpful Tips to Make Teaching Enjoyable

1. Close your eyes, take some deep, relaxing breaths and stretch your arms and legs. Get up from your chair and look out of the window for a full minute.
2. Get out of the room for a while and take a walk. In addition to getting some fresh air a change of scenery allows you to clear your mind a little.
3. Keep something nice on your desk such as fresh flowers, plants or photographs that will comfort you when you are feeling stressed.
4. Always switch off in the evenings. Do something enjoyable that doesn't involve teaching.
5. Give yourself realistic and attainable goals. Don't work just for the sake of working and always ask yourself what would be the worst thing to happen if you did not get a particular task done that day.
6. Eat well, and don't work through lunch. Give yourself some time off to look after yourself. Don't stock up on coffee and cigarettes, too many stimulants will only make you feel more grouchy and stressed out.
7. Seek help and guidance from colleagues and devise action plans to help everyone. Delegate work loads so that one person doesn't end up completely swamped with work. Share resources and lesson plans.
8. Try to spend time talking to the kids outside of lessons so you get to see them as people and not

just as students. Taking an active interest in the children you teach will help you put how they act in the classroom into perspective. It might also help them to see you as a person instead of just a teacher.

9. Keep happy. Smiling and laughing is good for you and will stop you feeling down or depressed. Seeing the funny side if things might be difficult, but it helps if you can have a laugh about something that has gone wrong instead of brooding over it.

10. Remember, you are a person, not just a teacher. Remind yourself of the reasons why you love your job, and not just because of the pay packet! Don't neglect your outside interests and keep at least one day of the week completely teaching free.

A happy and healthy teacher is likely to be a successful teacher. A stressed, irritable and tired teacher is not. You have a duty to yourself to look after your health and mental well-being. Never feel ashamed about asking for help if everything becomes too much. While teaching is a fantastic and very rewarding career, it is also only a job. A person who enjoys his or her job will be much better at it, than someone who does not.

10 Bringing it all Together

There are a huge number of factors to consider when looking at boys' underachievement and behaviour in schools: from how genetics determines how they look and act, to the possible special educational needs they may have; from the role models they see in society and their families, to the way they are taught in schools.

To pinpoint one reason and declare that to be the sole reason for boys' failing grades would be impossible and impractical, but as professional educators we need to be aware of, and understand, all the factors when attempting to address the problem.

People are like snowflakes, no two are ever completely alike, and with each storm there comes a new flurry of flakes. It is our job to try to make sure that we encourage and incorporate every individual in our teaching, pulling in the stragglers and the high achievers as one. There is no easy way; only time, patience and a willingness to learn ourselves will help us overcome the problems we face in the classroom. Good behaviour management takes determination and focus, and raising boys' achievement will never see an overnight solution.

While researching this book, I spoke to underachieving boys from four very different schools to build up a picture of the issues these boys face, and of what *they* thought were the problems and solutions.

Talking to the boys gave a unique insight into what they think are the causes of underachievement, and how they feel about school. Boredom and poor subject content were the top causes for not doing well in some classes, and badly managed behaviour issues by teachers were the main reasons why boys misbehaved.

The boys believed that being offered more vocational, skills-based classes would help them achieve better grades, and they would feel they were learning something useful. Being listened to was also important; some of the boys felt they were being talked down to, or that their opinion wasn't valued. All the boys commented on the fact that girls seemed to get more help in lessons, and that sometimes they didn't fully understand what they had to do.

Many boys said they felt trapped in their situation with no doors open to them, and that being in school was a complete waste of time. While getting good grades was recognized as important, over two-thirds of these boys had resigned themselves to achieving poor grades at GCSE and did not think they would continue to study post-16. Many had lost faith in the education system and thought it did nothing for them any more.

They were worried about finding a good job after school, and many thought they would probably end up claiming unemployment benefit or working in minimum wage jobs. Boys in lower sets felt they were in a catch-22 situation where they were stuck in lower ability classes and had no opportunity to achieve higher things. They were surrounded by other students of similar ability and they felt they had been put down in some way simply because they had not achieved high grades. They felt they were being judged from the moment they set foot in the classroom and that their teachers did not have high expectations of them.

Boys like these make up the current underachievement statistics. Although all of these boys were considered to be underachievers in schools, I know firsthand what these boys are capable of in many areas outside the classroom. One boy did not understand, nor could explain, what an adjective was, but he could fix an overhead projector in two minutes flat! Another boy was frequently excluded from lessons for bad behaviour and made to work in isolation, and yet when given the chance of work experience on a local farm he proved himself to be astounding when working with animals.

To raise boys' achievement, a holistic whole-school approach is needed. Adopting a cross-phase, community-wide approach means considering each attributing factor as an intrinsic piece of the wider picture. Strategies will only by effective if they are realistic and relevant and not all approaches will be successful in all schools for all students. Underachieving groups must be identified accurately, and any potential barriers that may hinder their progress must be cleared away. If these strategies and approaches are applied in a constant and informed way then the underachievement of boys could be effectively reduced, closing the achievement gap for good.

Boys' underachievement should never be justified. Although it can be explained, allowing it to continue would be a sign of bad practice by professional educators across the wider educational spectrum. With the many factors involved in this complicated issue, the problems have been recognized and accepted in the education profession. However, too much emphasis seems to be put on trying to justify it, rather than eradicating it. To prevent this issue affecting the future generations of boys, serious action needs to be taken by everyone in the education system to remove the problem for good.

By listening to our colleagues and sharing ideas, at the same time as listening to the boys themselves, we can find strategies that work. As teachers we are under great pressure to perform and succeed, and those pressures are multiplied a thousandfold for our students. While we have gone through our education and made our way in the world to some degree, these boys are still taking their first, crucial steps. What we teach them today is what they will use in the real world tomorrow.

Remember:

'I want to become a teacher because I want to try and make a difference to children's lives.'

With the right approach, attitude and dedication, you can.

Books, Articles and Websites

ADDISS, The National Attention Deficit Disorder Information and Support Service.
www.addiss.co.uk/index.html

Alexander, T. (1997) 'Learning Begins at Home – Implications for a Learning Society' in Cossin, B and Hales, M. *Families, Education and Social Differences.* London: Routledge.

Andrew, S. and Ross, C. (1988) *Boys Don't Cry: Boys and Sexism in Education.* Milton Keynes: Open University Press.

Arnold, R. (1997) *Raising Levels of Achievement in Boys.* Slough: NFER, EMI.

ATL Magazine (London).

BBC News Online Education website.
http://news.bbc.co.uk/1/hi/education/default.stm

Bleach, K. (ed.) (1998) *Raising Boys' Achievement in Schools.* London: Trentham Books Ltd.

Blum, P. (1998) *Surviving and Succeeding in Difficult Classrooms.* London: Routledge.

141

Chamberlain, D. B. (ed.) 'Prenatal Memory and Learning' Life Before Birth.
www.birthpsychology.com/lifebefore/early mem.html
Corrigan, P. (1979) *Schooling the Smash Street Kids.* London: Macmillan Education Ltd.
www.mirror.co.uk/news/allnews/tm_objectid
=14884745&method=full&siteid=50143&headline
=prince-charles–know-your-place-name_page.html
Duffy, M. (2002) 'The Achievement Gap'. *Times Educational Supplement,* 15 November.
Dunn, R. and Dunn, K. (2000) 'Learning styles: Theory, research, and practice', *National Forum of Applied Educational Research Journal,* 13 (1).
www.teresadybvig.com/learnsty.htm
Dunn, R., Burke, K. and Whitely, J. (2000) What Do You Know About Learning Styles? A Guide for Parents of Gifted Children (PHP).
www.nagc.org/Publications/Parenting/styles. html
Epstein, D., Elwood, J., Hey, V. and Maw, J. (eds) (1998) *Failing Boys? Issues in Gender and Achievement.* London: Open University Press.
Francis, B. (1999). 'Lads, lasses and (New) Labour 14–16-year-old students' responses to the laddish behaviour and boys' underachievement debate', *British Journal of Sociology of Education,* 20 (3), 355–71.
Francis, B. (2000). *Boys, Girls and Achievement: Addressing the Classroom Issues.* London: Routledge Falmer.
Gardner, H. (1993) *Frames of Mind: The Theory of Multiple Intelligences.* Second edition. London: Fontana:

Gregorc, A. F. (1982) Gregorc style delineator: *Development Technical and administration manual*. Massachusetts: Gabriel Systems Inc.

Head, J. (1999) *Understanding The Boys Issues of Behaviour and Achievement*. London: Falmer Press.

Holt, J. (1970) *How Children Learn*. London: Penguin Books.

Honey. P. and Mumford, A. (1992) *The Manual of Learning Styles*, Third Edition. Maidenhead: Peter Honey.

How Stuff Works.
www.howstuffworks.com

Kolb, D. A. (1976) *LSI – Learning Style Inventory: Technical Manual*. Boston: McBer.

Kolb, D. A. (1984) *Experiential Learning: experience as the source of learning and development*. New Jersey: Prentice Hall.

Kolb, D. A., Rubin, I. and McIntyre J. M. (eds) (1979) *Organisational psychology – A book of readings*. New Jersey: Prentice-Hall.

Moon, B. (ed:) (2002) *Teaching, Learning and the Curriculum in Secondary Schools*. London: Routledge Falmer.

Lane, D. A. (1990) *The Impossible Child*. Stoke-on-Trent: Trentham Books.

Manson, G. (1995) *Encouraging Your Child To Learn*. London: Macmillan Press.

Marks, J. (2001) *Girls Know Better: Educational Attainments of Boys and Girls*. London: CIVITAS: Institute for the Study of Civil Society.

McGivney, V. (1999) *Excluded Men – Men Who Are Missing from Education and Training* (National Institute of Adult Continuing Education)

McLellan, R. (2003) 'New Ways Of Thinking About Raising Boys' Achievement'. *Topic Online*, Autumn 2003, Issue 30.

McSherry, J. (2001) *Challenging Behaviours in Mainstream Schools: Practical Strategies for Effective Intervention and Reintegration*. London: David Fulton Publishers.

Millard, E. (1997) *Differently Literate: Boys, Girls and the Schooling of Literacy*. London: Falmer Press.

National Curriculum, The (1999). London: Department for Education and Employment and the Qualifications and Curriculum Authority.
Also http://www.hmso.gov.uk/guides.htm

National Literacy Trust, The.
www.literacytrust.org.uk/

National Statistics Online.
www.statistics.gov.uk

Patterson, J. (2004) 'The Rise of Teen Terrorists', *'Real' Magazine*, (10).

Renzulli, J. and Reis, S. M. (2000) 'The Schoolwide Enrichment Model'.
www.narragansett.k12.ri.us/NPS/faculty/Walsh/
enrich/2000-2001/page4.html

Rogers, B. (1995) *Behaviour Management – A Whole School Approach*. London: Paul Chapman.

Royal College of Psychiatrists, The.
www.rcpsych.ac.uk/